Holy Folly

SHORT AND TALL TALES FROM
THE ABBEY OF GETHSEMANI

Brother Paul Quenon, o.c.s.o.,

Brother Guerric Plante, o.c.s.o.,

Abbot Timothy Kelly, o.c.s.o.

Holy Folly

SHORT AND TALL TALES FROM THE ABBEY OF GETHSEMANI

Quenon, Paul

BLACK MOSS PRESS

BMP

1998

Published by Black Moss Press at 2450 Byng Road, Windsor, Ontario N8W 3E8, Canada.

Black Moss Press books are distributed in Canada and the U.S.
Firefly Books (U.S.) Inc.
P.O.Box 1338
Ellicott Station
Buffalo, New York 14207

Black Moss Press is grateful for grants under the Ontario Arts Council and the Department of Canadian Heritage.

Black Moss acknowledges the support of the Canada Council for the Arts for its publishing program.

CANADIAN CATALOGUING IN PUBLICATION DATA

Kelly, Timothy, 1935-
     Holy Folly

ISBN 0-88753-313-2

1. Abbey of Our Lady of Gethsemani (Trappist, Ky.)—Anecdotes. 2. Abbey of Our Lady of Gethsemani (Trappist, Ky.)—Sermons. I. Title.

PS8571.E58663H64 1998   C818'.5402   C98-900425-2
PR9199.3.K4168H64 1998

Cover photograph is from the Abbey of Gethsemani archives.
Back cover photographs were supplied by Brother Paul Quenon.
Cover design by John Doherty.

INTRODUCTION

It was shortly after Christmas in 1961, a year after I completed my novitiate with Father Louis (Merton), when I was invited by the Prior and Master of Scholastics to go with them to his hermitage for a Christmas visit. We sat in front of the fireplace and exchanged community gossip, and later as we were returning through the woods for Vespers, Father Louis launched into an animated description, with arms sweeping the air, of the blunt old monk Father Idesbald. In the Infirmary Refectory an audio tape had been loudly played of a speech by an over-zealous liturgists. Idesbald abruptly got up and went through the door with a bang. His neighbor, old hunched Father Stephen, whose communications with hand signs were always accompanied by whispers, and whose whispers lapsed into a whistle, flashed a hand sign: "O, he's-ss dead in the ears-ss!"

Father Louis used to say that if he ever wrote a novel about the monastery, these are the people he would write about. The task has not yet found its novelist and perhaps never will, since the fulsome literary form of a novel is alien to the brevity of monastic lore. Usually one could put in a few cartoon frames the stories about monks, especially the classical tales of the ancient Desert Fathers — each one memorable and ending with a punch: A devout Judge comes from Alexandria to find Abba Moses, and encounters an wild looking man in black speeding by. He inquires after Abba Moses and is told: "What do you want with that mad man and heretic?" On arriving at the monastery he learns that wild man himself was Moses.

Final Frame: He returns to town feeling he's had his money's worth.

That is not too different from a story told by Father Timothy Kelly, the present Abbot of Gethsemani, about Father Louis when Father Timothy had his first interview upon arriving at the monastery. He did not know the Novice Master himself was Merton and mentioned reading Merton books. "Well," he asked, "what do you think of them?" "I think they are a bit romantic." he said. "Yes," he replied, "you have to watch out what you read."

This makes me think of another...but I am getting ahead of myself. I first have to put in a word about the inexcusable habit monks have of telling stories about one another. This book is, on my part at least, an example of such a reprehensible practice which, however, is as old as monasticism itself.

To say the word monk is to say the word silence, the word solitude. But the irony of history is that there is in an inexhaustible literature of monastic tales, and for the most part these were tales generated and passed on by monks and nuns themselves. If monks were always so silent, how is it we have so many stories about them? From the beginning stories were told about them, and by them. Word would travel from cell to cell of some sage remark or remarkable deed, and this in turn passed from generation to generation in a very active oral tradition. Visiting scribes recorded this accumulation which became, for instance, the Institutes and Conferences of Cassian, or the Lausiac History of Palladius, to name some of the prominent among many collections.

Certainly speech in the daily life of monks had its restrictions: "Calumny, empty talk, nattering, and low-grade clowning" were forbidden, (but not altogether absent); speech was to be used for the upbuilding of charity and for imparting received wisdom. Indeed this was the very motivation behind the abundant collections of words and deeds of the Fathers and Mothers of the Desert. The living wisdom and charity, born of purity of heart, was the gospel of the desert.

But wisdom proves more convincing when presented in its human embodiment, and sometimes that embodiment is like dross that hides a grain of gold. The gold makes the whole lump a unique discovery.

Stories and proverbs continue to create themselves daily in monasteries. You need only pay a little attention to catch one before it passes by and is forgotten entirely. Usually the community kitchen is a foremost clearing house for such exchanges in a monastery. I know because I cooked at Gethsemani from 1973 to 1997. I am not much of a storyteller myself. Most of what is written here are things I've overheard, material borrowed from the telling and retelling that takes place while peeling potatoes or shaving carrots with two or three other monks. Occasionally I get an urge to write something down, but I am far from consistent in my writing habits. Thus there are large time gaps and little sequence in what I have recorded.

Below a thin surface of uniformity, monks are unique and singular. You want both to admire them and strangle them at the same time. Monks described here may appear out of the ordinary but in fact they have their counterparts in many other monasteries. They are not so rare as they might seem.

Authority in recent years has renewed its cautions against individualism, but the unavoidable fact is that monasteries draw "the loners" to begin with. A person leaves home, family, and the conventions of society to enter a community that functions by modes and standards different from, and even at odds with, whatever prevailed in their lives before. A man or woman has to break with what is taken for granted, including the worldly conventions about how to realize your own individuality. A redefinition of self takes place in the monastery, and more often than not the result corresponds neither to the accepted community model (discipline, regularity, obedience) nor to the ideals recognized by the world. Somewhere in the process the Spirit does a creative innovation — or maybe human nature just makes another one of its inexhaustible expressions. In any case, an untold wealth of characters, personalities and stories results. This collection only scratches the surface of what might be found in the monastic world.

In part one, Holy Folly, I make no pretenses of writing hagiography and wish to canonize nobody. If anything, for the sake of realism I focus on the disedifying, irregular and unexemplary situations, confident that in these human interactions, and even infractions of discipline, some grain of priceless gold flashes, however briefly.

Since, even with our Trappist emphasis on enclosure, the monastery's neighborhood and its social context is an integral part of its life, I include stories about the interaction of monks with "outsiders," which in the long run reveal the truth of what is truly "inside" the monks concerned.

Part two is by Brother Guerric who was a story-teller by temperament. He strongly preferred the spoken word and a live listener. He had a limitless string of tales to tell. Only just before his death he started to make the effort to translate them into writing, a form he was just beginning to develop. He was only one of several monks I have known who embody an extraordinary wealth of lore and experience.

Part Three is excerpts from the funeral orations of our Abbot Timothy, who strikes a delicate balance between what is upbuilding for the liturgical occasion and what is honest and true to the human character being commemorated. The result is miniatures, which are remarkable for their truth of portrayal, depth of understanding and compassion. They are also unique in their perspective as of a pastor who knows by name those who until their last breath often remained an enigma for all of us.

—*Brother Paul Quenon*
Abbey of Gethsemani, Trappist, Ky.

PART ONE

HOLY FOLLY

BROTHER PAUL QUENON

HOLY FOLLY

December 31, 1983—

The old irrepressible Brother Octavius comes into the kitchen after having spent many days in the Infirmary because of a fall, and is greeted by everyone: "Look, he's back on his feet!"

"It is because I am German. The Germans are wonderful people, yes!"

He wanted something sweet. I showed him a can of cookies that came in the mail for Brother Claude, and offered him some. He said: "No, you give to me. I cannot take in my hand, it is not enough. Put it in a bowl."

Someone teased him: "Look at all you are taking! You're a pig!"

"Yes, I am a pig. The biggest one. Pigs are better. They are the most expensive on the market."

✝✝✝

Brother Columban tells me the fad in Nelson County for Christmas entertainment this year is Indian wrestling. Instead of playing bridge or singing carols, the men lay down side by side in opposite positions and try to flip one another with a leg. The wives make bets and cheer.

✝✝✝

January 3, 1984—

Brother Victor told me of the change in a certain Brother after what they perceived as the suppression of the way of life of the lay brothers by the General Chapter of the 1960s. Formerly this Brother had been such a cordial, cooperative and compliant person, but afterwards he was always ready for a fight and opposed authority on everything. He eventually left the monastery.

Brother Victor told him: "I agree with the same things you are mad about, but there is no use getting mad. It is over and done with! Authority has spoken." But the Brother was not to be consoled. As they were driving back from Louisville, Brother was fuming and cussing. Brother Victor rolled down the window.

"It's cold! What are you doing that for?" asked the Brother.

"I'm letting some of the blue air out of here." Victor shot back.

I tell Victor: "That is what happens when people are too compliant to begin with. They end up going to the opposite extreme."

He said: "That's why I don't have ulcers. When I get mad I blow my top, and that's the end of it."

✝✝✝

January 4, 1984—

Some pipes broke last week in the vacated Retreat House, because it was left unheated. Today a pipe broke alongside the tunnel. Charlie Boon was called in to dig with his backhoe, which crouches like Behemoth the Dragon outside the entrance. The basement is filled with sulfuric fumes of sewer gas. Will the night be filled with phantoms?

✝✝✝

January 6, 1984—

Brother Andrew, one of the cooks, tells me when things used to disappear from the ice box, they would always assume the culprit was Father Idesbald (now deceased). About age 80-going-on-14, he would take generously from the plates and trays prepared for others with their names on it. One day Brother Maurice, a cook, walked into the kitchen and found Father Idesbald peering into the refrigerator. Maurice gave him a swat on the rear. Idesbald grabbed a butcher knife and brandished it at Maurice. When Andrew walked into the kitchen, Maurice was backed up against the oven laughing uncontrollably.

14

January 7, 1984—

Jeff Fagenbush, a young temporary resident, has decided to give up his comic books. The inspiration came to him suddenly, during Mass, and he turned over the whole collection to Brother Anthony — a collection he has assembled over many years. In the world of comic book collectors, it would be worth much. Jeff was baptized the Sunday before Christmas. He has been at the monastery since early November. He lives in the vacated Retreat House, and works with Brother Ambrose in the kitchen, as well as in the Farms Building where cheese is packed.

Jeff is a 23. He was kicked out of every year of school he attended since 6th grade, the year his father left home. He has been in prison, and now is a fugitive from the law. Brother Ambrose has been helping him and his older brother, John Joseph, for years, getting them out of trouble. Now he has them both baptized. The change in Jeff since coming here has been noticeable, although he still likes to wear tight patchy jeans.

So who has the comics? I do. I got them from Anthony. Now you know the worst about me.

John Joseph Fagenbush, the older brother of Jeff, came here first with his uncle, a truck driver. John did not have the faintest idea of what kind of a place a monastery might be. He had never even heard of the term. The sign at the entry gate particularly frightened him: NO ENTRANCE UNDER PAIN OF EXCOMMUNICATION. He had no idea what excommunication meant. All he knew is that it didn't sound good — like you might get shot. His uncle drove him up, opened the gate, backed up, then bolted forward at full roar past the threatening sign. John yelled: "Hey! this isn't funny anymore, stop!" and ducked beneath the dashboard.

They went to the cheese packaging to make the regular mail delivery. That is where John first met Ambrose. He began asking him questions, and when he asked what a monk is, Ambrose explained how the word comes from the Greek word *monos*, meaning alone. "Monks are called that because they live in solitude." John said: "You are not alone because you live with God." After that, Ambrose took real interest in John.

At Christmas time Ambrose sent him a Gethsemani Farms fruitcake, and invited him back. John did not respond. He said: "I figured all those monks are queer and someone was liable to grab me." His Grandma told him he ought to at least go back and thank Ambrose. He did. After that, the visits were more frequent, especially since there was livestock and things rare for a young man from the city.

Once Ambrose was called out to handle a neighbor's horse, that was in heat and particularly difficult to control. John, hearing new words, got them tangled up in describing the animal to two of our hired men from neighboring farms:

"Yes sir, that was a mean old stud-mare."

They howled and said: "I'd be mean too, if I was a stud-mare!"

At that time Jeff, John's brother, had blond hair down to his waist, and could not stand staying around the monastery more than 2 or 3 days.

Both of the Fagenbush boys seem devoted to their Grandma. She is a lovable person, who was the best influence they ever had. She says she can raise a garden as good as any man, smokes incessantly, and wheezes badly. She married three times, and can take care of herself. She will, by their account, use a skillet on the side of a man's head if she wants to.

It was thanks to her that John and Jeff were put in jail. They had robbed a liquor store, returned home and got drunk on the takings. Soon they got into a brawl, and Grandma called the police.

Her husband killed her son (the father of John and Jeff) in order to stop a fit of violence. Jeff thus witnessed the murder of his own dad. His father had been prevented from visiting his own children, and had become so irate that Grandma had to flee to a neighbor's. And when he tired to pursue her he was stopped with a shot in the back.

✝✝✝

One reason Ambrose is so devoted to the poor is that he was so poor himself. As a child of a Mexican family, he had lived in a house with a mud floor. All might have died of typhoid if a Baptist minister had not found them and helped them out. They were poor, but had dignity. When Ambrose's sister came back from the store one day with more money than she had gone with — the clerk had given the wrong change — their mother made her go back and return it, even though that was all the money they had in the house.

Ambrose will do almost anything to help the poor, including using the monastery's resources to do it — much to the chagrin of the Cellerar and Department Heads. One day the Cobbler found all the boots missing from the shoe shop. It took no time to guess where they might have gone. When approached, Ambrose answered: "Why should the monks be wearing $40 shoes when a family in the neighborhood has no shoes at all?"

The fact the boots would not fit the kids was of no consequence to him. He had them stuff paper in the toes and heels.

The electrician keeps his shop carefully locked against Ambrose, and speaks of him as "Robin Hood."

There was one time when it seemed to Ambrose we had too many toilets, and much to the dismay of the plumber, one disappeared from what is euphonically called The Grand Parlor. He had taken it to a poor neighbor who was building a new house.

Unfortunately for me because that particular toilet was my favorite.

✝✝✝

January 10, 1984—

Father Timothy, the Abbot, has acquired a reputation for being an axe man in the Cistercian Order, having been instrumental in the retirement of two Abbots. Today he announced he must go to Iowa to conduct an election for the Abbot at New Melleray. Father David, the current Abbot, has decided not to accept re-election. This is not to Father Timothy's liking. "For once," he says, "I would rather re-install an Abbot than depose him."

✝✝✝

January 15, 1984—

Today Ambrose and Jeff had an accident on the way to Louisville. They were going to see Jeff's Grandmother. Full details have not come in yet, except that it was a two car collision and Ambrose is in the hospital.

Perhaps this is the final culmination in a whole history of calamities involving Ambrose, cars and the Fagenbush boys. The last time something happened, it resulted in Brother Ambrose going to jail.

At that time, Ambrose's white hair was down to his shoulders, and his white beard, half way down his chest. After living through long years of the regulation cropped hair, he took advantage of the new air of freedom of the 1970s. He decided to look just the way God had made him.

This did not help him one day when he was taking Jeff to visit a friend in prison. He was stopped by the police for speeding. When asked for his license he couldn't produce it. Ambrose had no license to his name because the Abbot forbade him to get one. Too frequently he was gone from the enclosure and off to some poor farmhouse without permission. So this was an effort of the Abbot to keep him at home. Not to any great avail! Now, Ambrose was faced with a policeman and a charge of speeding. He told the policeman he was from the monastery, thinking this might spare him. The cop looked at Ambrose, at the rough appearance of the kid with hair reaching to his waist, then answered: "The monks wear their beards short, I'm taking you to jail."

When the Judge called the Abbot to inquire whether, indeed, this Ambrose was one of the monks, he learned he was. The Judge offered to write off the charge and release him. However, Father Timothy said: "No sir. You treat him to the usual procedures."

When Timothy got to town, he found Ambrose in jail, as he requested. But the Judge released him anyhow.

Another occasion of the ill-starred conjunction of Ambrose, cars and Fagenbush boys, was when the garage almost caught fire. John Joseph had been here almost seven months. In order to help him get a job, and set himself up in the world, the Abbot decided to buy him a vehicle. John's friends advised him to get a pick-up truck, but he wanted nothing else but a passenger car. So the monastery got him a used two door yellow Mustang. John and Ambrose worked on it in the garage to get it running properly. At one point, Ambrose was holding a flashlight over the gas tank when it slipped from his hand and fell in, somehow igniting the gas. The fire detectors should have set off an alarm immediately, but nothing happened. Ambrose pulled the hand alarm. Still there was no sound. He went to another building, pulled a signal there, then to another, and another.

It so happened I had been repairing the alarm system that day and forgot to turn it back on!

John, ran to find Brother Jacob, the monastery fire chief, to bring the fire truck. People started gathering at the garage where smoke billowed forth. After some delay the fire truck still had not appeared. Fortunately, someone had the presence of mind to push the car out of the garage. The fire was then extinguished with chemicals. Damage was done to the garage door, but not the ceiling. The car was no longer usable.

The ancient and seldom used fire truck never did appear because Jacob could not get it started. It was a small, well guarded relic which, on rare occasions, filled the entire enclosure area with a roar equal to a truck three times its size. In its dim past it once had a sacredness equivalent to the ark of the covenant. A former Abbot publicly forbade anyone to touch it under pain of sin, just to assure its proper protection. Soon afterward someone scrawled in its thick coating of dust: "I SINNED."

John's car was eventually replaced by one of the monastery pickups.

†††

News has arrived that the accident with Ambrose and Jeff today was quite serious. The two were just beyond the bridge going towards Bardstown when a car crossed the center line and smashed into our pickup. The man inside was killed. He must have blacked out at the wheel because he never applied his brakes. Jeff hurt his feet, but no bones were broken. Ambrose is in the hospital at the University of Louisville with a broken ankle and a torn larynx.

When Jeff saw Ambrose lying on the seat and blood coming out of his mouth, he asked: "Ambrose, are you all right?"

Ambrose gurgled back: "Yea, I'm all right."

When the ambulance arrived they found Ambrose standing outside the car, directing traffic around the wreckage with one hand, and holding his larynx together with the other.

It is hard to know what will happen to Jeff now. He was driving, and had no license. The permit he carried was his brother's, and that was expired. This has not been detected yet —J. Fagenbush covers for both John and Jeff. If they do find out who he is they will take him to court. He has other matters to settle with the law, and there will be big trouble.

†††

January 16, 1984—

Jeff has returned to the monastery, and I visited his room in the infirmary. He has a strong build and looks all right, but he must have suffered internal shock from the impact. By gripping the steering wheel tightly, he had protected himself by sheer power of his arms.

This has been quite a turn of events for Jeff, since he was about to end his time at the monastery and continue his flight from the law. However, this was hardly his first concern. When he saw me, he wept: "I did not want to hurt Ambrose!"

†††

January 29, 1984—

After this nearly fatal accident, Ambrose is besieged with visitors at the hospital. When Father Timothy arrives, he finds people about to leave, and when he leaves more are arriving. During Saturday afternoon confessions, neighbors stop in the middle of their confessions to ask about Ambrose. The monk is well known because of the years he cared for horses, and for his skill in mechanics and farming.

His way with animals is extraordinary. Once, the brothers decided to rent out our prize winning bull, Orbiter, for breeding. They, and the customer, had spent an hour trying to get the monster into a trailer for transportation. In final desperation, they phoned Ambrose in the kitchen. He walked half a mile to the cow barn, took the rope on the bull, led him into the trailer, and closed the door behind. Simple as that! He then walked back to the kitchen, leaving them quite in awe.

For this, and other reasons Brother Malachy calls him Doctor X. Also for his ingenious mechanical inventions, his mysterious repairs, and his unpredictable concoctions in the salad department: Jello salad with an inch and a half of meringue, spiked with rum, enchiladas that continue to announce their flavor five hours after consumption, fermented fruit juice that immediately causes a band of constriction across the upper abdomen.

20

Brother Ambrose

†††

Jeff is in a precarious state of affairs now. He is avoiding the law. Ambrose has decided to keep him in hiding because he considers imprisonment the most demoralizing alternative for Jeff. After being away for more than a year — having left Kentucky at Ambrose's instigation — he's come back to the monastery. Jeff had been on parole and could not find a job in Kentucky. Ambrose judges idleness more undesirable than jumping parole. That's why he urged him to go to Texas for a new job. Now Jeff is back. The law is likely to have little sympathy with him. The fact is, it was all in accordance with Ambrose's advice.

Says the Abbot: "That man!"

†††

Brother Casper is scarcely eating anymore. No apparent reason, except he is missing his bottom row of teeth, and is so feeble.

†††

February 1, 1984—

I went to Bardstown and photographed the wrecked pickup, which is deeply stoved in. The windshield, where Ambrose hit his head, is a bulge with a tear in it, the glass a spider web.

Today they brought Ambrose home from the hospital. He wanted badly to return, knowing the room in the hospital was over $1000 a day! He stayed three weeks, whereas others with a less complicated condition would stay six to eight weeks.

The community has not heard of all the sufferings he has been enduring: Sleeplessness, because he coughs as soon as he begins to drift off. Hallucination: "I know what drug trips are like now." "For three days I had a total, excruciating pain. I couldn't localize where it was."

I said: "The hallucination might have come from wanting to get out of your body."

He said: "Yes, and I had an out-of-the-body experience. It was a feeling of lightness. I don't know where I was, but the body with its pain was not there. And it seemed like our Lord, or someone, was there. I felt I was being lifted up and it lasted all night. After that, the pain was no longer so great for me." (or did I hear him say: "No longer greater than me")?

The doctor had told him that unless a Higher Power was behind him, he would never have pulled through.

Ambrose had also developed pneumonia, and ran a temperature of 103 which they were unable to control.

About Jeff, he said: "He is immature and has many things to get over, but down deep he is with God."

The Berry family, the family of the man killed in the accident, did not have insurance on the car since he was epileptic. His accident was apparently caused by a black out. We also will not be able to collect insurance, since the driver was unlicensed. The Abbot told the family not to worry about paying for damages. They do not have too much. The man had one child, one adopted child, another on the way.

✝✝✝

February 11, 1984—

During the Night Office the door of the upper half of the organ fell to the floor. The choir did not miss a beat and continued the psalmody as smoothly as ever.

✝✝✝

When Brother Octavius goes to a hospital he tells the nurse: "I came all the way from Cologne, the most beautiful city in the world, and came all the way to this country, and entered this hospital just so you could take care of me."

✝✝✝

Jeff has gone to the Abbot, Father Timothy, and said he is willing to serve time in prison if it is not too long. This will take some doing, since Jeff has twenty years hanging over his head. The Abbot has engaged our lawyer. There will be a trial this week. He has Jeff out on a $10,000 bail, which in fact involves only $1,000 in payment. Says Jeff to me: "You'll have to do some heavy-duty praying this Friday."

The accident certainly changed the course and direction of events. Ambrose was planning to send Jeff away the week of the accident. At the scene of the accident Jeff kept asking, with sobs: "Why did this happen now?" They had been praying the rosary as they were driving. Ambrose himself had been thanking God for his quiet life as a contemplative —!!!

When presented with Jeff's insistent question, "Why now?" Ambrose said: "You have to believe it is ultimately to increase your love of God and intimacy with Christ."

†††

February 14, 1984—

Now Ambrose is getting around the monastery on a walker, and goes to the kitchen to make the community salad as usual. Says Brother Claude: "Look at that! and when Brother Roland broke his little toe he didn't move for six months."

†††

Last Sunday former Brother Wenceslaus, Jeff, Brother Harold, and I hiked up to the hermitage on top of the northernmost knob. Jeff and I misbehaved all afternoon: Throwing rocks, punching, swinging on vines, wrestling. "But no cussing allowed," said Harold). The monks are generally too gentle. It was refreshing for everybody to carry on this way for a change.

†††

February 16, 1984—

Brother Victor tells me if I ever want to get out of the kitchen job, which I don't, I should serve rice or noodles every day. That is how he did it himself. When he was cook in the '50s potatoes became very expensive. Dom James, then Abbot, did not have enough money to buy them, so Victor served rice or macaroni daily. Dom James did not want to face the discontent of the community, and Victor, for his own reasons, did not mind the discontent at all. So the two made an agreement: Whenever anyone would complain to Dom James, he would send them down to the kitchen to report their complaint to Victor. (A formidable prospect to face!) Victor would say: "Why blame me? I have no word personally from the Abbot to serve potatoes. Show it to me in writing." When they went back to get the written statement and knocked on the Abbot's door, he would not answer.

Victor knew by the time it was all over there would be unanimous consent to have him removed from the kitchen. He could smile at criticism because he badly wanted out.

In fact, he ended up going from one cooking job to another. His latter days in the kitchen were spent in devising a recipe for cheese. This eventually became his job, and the mainstay of Gethsemani's economy.

24

✝✝✝

February 22, 1984—

Today when Brother Camillus was pouring the soup someone remarked on how thin it was. He replied: "This is Third World soup."

✝✝✝

The weather is already like March, and I took a bicycle ride with Father Matthew Kelty. He pointed out the place where a home of one of our workers burnt down some 20 years ago. They had no telephone to call the fire truck. Since the husband was not home, the wife put the children in the car and hurried to the monastery to rouse our fire truck for action.

But Dom James would not send out our fire truck. He had a strict rule against it: "What if we should have a fire while the truck was missing?"

So Brother Victor filled up the portable watering tank for the garden and rushed to the fire. Of course, by the time he arrived, it was too late. Everything was lost except the laundry on the clothes line. Brother Conrad saw the propane tank was dangerously close to the fire, walked right up, disconnected it and shoved it out of harms way.

It was not a matter of indifference to the poor neighbors in those days. We had food lines at the door every Wednesday that reached to the end of the avenue — but there was a strange way of slicing the pie to fit the rules.

✝✝✝

February 27, 1984—

Well, the court trials are over. Jeff has to spend 90 days in the county jail, which is a light sentence considering the fact that he had 20 years hanging over his head. There were two trials. At the first, they gave him a one year sentence, suspended for 2 years. This means he does not have to go to jail unless he gets into trouble within that period. At the second trial this week, he was given time for jumping parole, which he has done twice.

Father Timothy went on the stand many times for Jeff. No doubt that is why he got such a light sentence. I do think Jeff really wants to change and has already. He is elated over the short term, and says he could spend the three months standing on his head if he had to.

March 1, 1984—

A few weeks after Ambrose got home from the hospital he wanted to make public apologies in Chapter for all the trouble he has caused. He asked the Abbot if he could, but the Abbot preferred to convey the message to us for him.

The Abbot emphasized we should not encourage Ambrose in his ways or make a hero out of him. Under these circumstances this sounded harsh, but the fact is Ambrose needs protection. He goes through cycles where he gets himself into a knot helping out some needy person. He becomes so tense he must retreat to bed with migraines.

Brother Columban is skeptical about apologies from Ambrose. Says we should be warned if he starts making apologies. That is a sure sign he is about to pull another stunt. When Columban worked with him at the cow barn, Ambrose would pull off some incredible stunt, get the whole crew mad, then return with elaborate apologies. The apology was only a sign that as soon as they turned their backs he would go and pull another one.

Brother Jacob suggested Ambrose ought to write a book entitled: "How To Do Good And Get Everybody Mad."

✝✝✝

Today Jeff has left for jail. I walked into his empty room to retrieve things he left behind. Up from the bed jumps a young man. He is James Reed, another ex-convict Ambrose had invited from Blackburn and LaGrange.

✝✝✝

Evening

For the first time in the history of our monastery, a group of women ate in our community refectory. They were the Cistercian nuns, here for the Regional Meeting of the Order. I sat with Mother Miriam from Redwoods Monastery, who paused for a moment in the conversation because she wanted to absorb, she said, "the atmosphere of the place where so many monks for so many years ate and listened to the reading, laughed and performed public penance." (The refectory was scene for certain penances assigned for an offense, such as eating in the middle of the room, under the eyes of all, seated on a very low stool.)

During our meals a book is publicly read over the microphone. I told her the story of the time one of the innocent souls doing the reading from a biography of St.Jerome, came upon the episode of Jerome's sexual temptations. The monk read a passage describing St. Jerome having a fantasy about being locked, he read, in a garden full of "courtesans," except that he pronounced it "Cartesians." Everyone was discreetly silent until one lone voice from the adjoining Infirmary Refectory let out a yelp of laughter. We all assumed it was Father Louis, for he ate in the Infirm Refectory. Father Louis however claimed it was Brother Fidelis. Brother Fidelis in turn claimed it was Father Louis.

†††

March 11, 1984—

Ambrose's friend, James Reed, went home today to Beaver Dam Ky. In prison his name was Goober. He seemed sad to leave, he liked it here.

Yesterday at work in the kitchen he kept his leg propped up on a stool, and limped when he walked. I asked him what happened. He said he was walking along the road to New Haven, and some driver nearly knocked him off the road. Goober swore at him, and the guy stopped the car and got out to fight. He was drunk. The two got to tussling, and the man kicked Goober in the shins with his hard toe boot. In the end Goober, a rather short guy, got the better of him and had the man pinned down. The fellow got in his car and drove away. Goober hitched a ride to the monastery: "Strange neighborhood here!"

He seems such a gentle fellow. I'm sure he will be back.

†††

March 17, 1984—

For several weeks now Ambrose has been out of the leg cast, but is having much pain. He holds the tip of his tongue to his upper tooth when he takes a step.

He said James Reed phoned and said he has almost decided to become a monk.

†††

June 10, 1984—

Jeff Fagenbush was released from jail. He got a job in Louisville, but quit it. Then he came here. After a week or so,

Father Timothy got him a construction job with a neighbor. On the first day Jeff would not take warning about wearing a shirt under the bright sun and got a severe sunburn. He could not sleep all night, and did not go to work the next day. So the boss gave him a check for a day's work and fired him. We haven't seen Jeff since. He got away fast before Ambrose could give him a piece of his mind.

✝✝✝

Kind of a koan: Can the middle class mediocre American male find God?

✝✝✝

January 24, 1985—
Father Francis Klein was ordained to the office of Reader and Acolyte today. I noticed after today's dinner although he was not finished eating when the concluding bell rang, he got up and helped clear the tables.

✝✝✝

There is a fat bandage on Ambrose's finger. He explained how a machine tried to take off his finger but did not succeed.

It seems a machine makes an assault on him once a year. Like the time when a post hole drill grabbed his work robe and pulled him into the machinery. His buttocks were severely lacerated, and he had to be stitched. That was when Dom James decided the monks should no longer wear work robes but trousers instead.

Or there was the time at one of the out buildings, Ambrose was using a power saw, cut his hand, and left a trail of blood a block long to the infirmary.

Still, he has a genius for machinery, and can construct one out of scrap material for whatever purpose. The old machine used for shrink wrapping the cheese was his invention.

✝✝✝

March 18, 1985—
On the feast of St.Patrick it is *de rigeur* to serve something green for dinner. One item is Ambrose's green jello-fruit-cheese mix topped with meringue seasoned with Creme du Mint. When he failed to produce that as usual this year, I asked why: "I'll serve it tomorrow for the Solemnity of St.Joseph — he was Irish anyhow."

28

July 4, 1986—

A conversation, in mock solemn tones, overheard before dinner:

Alfred: "What hath Ambrose wrought today? Is it healthy or otherwise?"

Guerric: "He offered me a drink of it, but I told him I didn't need to be cleaned out today. He said he started it with grape juice."

Alfred: "Now Brother, we must make an effort to be charitable towards our Brother in all circumstances."

Guerric: "That was not meant to injure, I was only expressing the way I felt."

Alfred: "Sometimes it takes a special effort."

Guerric: "Now, what could I have done in this circumstance to preserve charity?!!"

The "cider," as he calls it, was a nice rose color, and indeed formidable.

✝✝✝

August 1, 1986—

Not very long ago I held a baby in my arms who was alive due to the intervention of Brother Ambrose. The baby's name is Cody and is the son of a young man, Claude, from Bardstown. The mother is Norma Jean, who previously had a child by Jeff. That is how Ambrose came to know her.

When she was pregnant again, still unmarried and living with this jobless father. Ambrose became the man of the hour. He hired Claude in the kitchen, and found a residence — the "solar house," located just beyond our boundary and owned by Bellarmine College.

Claude is dark and has a lean appeal, but somehow his looks change daily. He spent time in prison a good while ago, and is now making salads in the monastery. Norma Jean wanted to have an abortion, but with some persuasion Ambrose got her to agree to adoption. He set her up at some hospice in another state where care and delivery would be provided. She went there, but the only hitch was that she was expected to work! So she decided to leave and returned to Kentucky.

She delivered the baby in June. The couple has a temporary home, an old station wagon and a dismantled truck.

✝✝✝

January 2, 1987—

The Grand Parlor, where the community showers are located, was evacuated for renovation. That now means the shower and tub on the second floor north will have increased use. The custodian, Father Matthew, posted this notice:

New Patrons!

Welcome to our facility!

If you shower with the curtains inside the tub, the water will not run onto the floor.

If it does so run, mop it, for it tends to end as a stain on the scriptorium ceiling. You've noticed?

May as well tell you, the high pressure water line runs the length of this corridor. It makes much noise. So showering after bedtime will not win you friends and may lose you some.

Until we have a better world -

Matthew,

Custos.

✝✝✝

According to the Rule of St. Benedict, a monk has no claims of ownership over anything, not even over his own body. This was put to the test in a rather literal way for Father Matthew. This, by his own account, is what happened:

"I went to renew my drivers license in Bardstown. At the bottom of the sheet a question: 'Do you want to will your body to Science?'"

"I thought: Not a bad idea!"

"So I filled out the form. And forgot about it."

"Weeks later, in casual converse with the Abbot: 'By the way, I gave my body to Science.'"

"'No you didn't. You have no jurisdiction over your body.'"

"The Loretto nuns (neighbors) do it. And any way, it's all done."

"'Well, go and undo it.'"

"So I had to go back to the woman and get my body back. 'I have no jurisdiction over it,' I told her."

March 18, 1987—

Brother Owen is old and hard working. He is the mop and bucket man in the cheese processing department, and is obsessively sanitary. He will pull up the hem of his house robe to open a doorknob with hand covered. One of his rituals of purification is his preparation for breakfast, which begins 15 minutes before most of the monks are awake.

He first selects his plates carefully from the stack, removing one from the middle, since the top or bottom may have been fingered. Dust will have spoiled the top plate. He then gets his bread, again, from the middle of the stack, since top may be dry or dusty, the middle fresh and untouched. Next comes the elaborate coffee mug routine. Selecting one of the stainless steel, quart size mugs, he fills it once with scalding water from the coffee dispenser, pours it out, fills it a second time and pours that out. Then he fills it with coffee, pours the coffee down the drain and fills the cup a second time, and again pours it out. This way he gets his coffee from the middle of the tank, which drains from the bottom, or at least eliminates the dregs and debris that might exist there. Finally, he gives the cup one more full rinse with hot water, and then draws the last cup of coffee, safe, uncontaminated, perfect.

Back in the days when the only warm shower in the monastery was in one special suite in the Retreat House, Owen would go every Sunday morning at 6:00 and enter the suite, whether it was occupied or not. He would make reassuring signs to any occupant and proceed to the shower to get his warm weekly wash.

†††

November 19, 1987—

I asked Brother Tobias (86 years old) if he will be the next one in the community to die. He said: "I've been dead for six years."

Ever since his heart attack six years ago he has been living from day to day, never knowing when he goes to bed, whether he will wake up again. He found the medicine given him too strong, and decided not to take it.

"That was six years ago, and look, I'm still alive! I'm ready to die any time." This, he said, peering up at me with his gray-green eyes.

April 10, 1988—

Brother Victor told me about the first time he saw Brother Ambrose. Victor entered the monastery after a group, including Ambrose, had been sent to Georgia, in 1946, to found a new monastery. Ambrose was sent as the Cellarer, since Dom James felt he could swear by the man. The community had to live there in drafty barns until the monastery was built. But Ambrose was determined to make it economically viable first and foremost. So he hit on the idea that a monastery in the peach state could survive by canning peaches. He went out and bought boxcar loads of peaches. The monks were so pressed to complete the canning there was no time to build the monastery.

In due time, reports were circulating at Gethsemani that Ambrose was returning. The brothers were warning Victor: "Watch out, he's coming back, there'll be trouble!"

"And when I finally saw him I said: 'What? That little guy! That's what they are all worried about?'"

"They couldn't sell the canned peaches in Georgia, so Gethsemani bought them. That is why we were eating canned peaches for the next five years."

Such at least is Victor's rendition of the legend. Brother Guerric informs me that the inexhaustible canned peaches were thanks to our own Interior Cellarer, who would buy them by the truck load and can them locally.

✝✝✝

February 3, 1989—

Ambrose is put out with James (Goober) Reed. He shakes his head and says: "No."

James was here through much of the Advent and Christmas season. He was out of prison again. He did not have a job yet. One day James looked at me and said in his shy, boy-like way: "I might be joining the monastery. It's not what I want, but it's what God wants."

Fred Boone, a shrewd young neighbor, noticed James at Compline one night with a rosary in each hand, his eyes closed, his head raised to the ceiling.

I told Fred he wants to enter the monastery. He said: "That boy is lookin' for a ride on the gravy train."

James was having the regular interviews with the Vocational Directors. The upshot of it was they thought it would not be good for him to enter now. He should get a job first and set himself up in the world. Then, if he wants to enter the monastery his motive will be less ambiguous.

James complied and went to Lexington to get a job. Ambrose gave him money to rent an apartment. After a few weeks he was evicted. He brought homeless people in off the street, and would let them spend the night in his apartment.

Ambrose and Brother Frederic went to visit him after the eviction and found him living in some run down housing. Ambrose could not believe people can live in such squalor. He gave James another $250 to rent a better place. Meanwhile, James had lined up a good job working at McDonald's. Everything seemed fine, it looked as if everything was going to turn out all right.

But then James found he could use the $250 to buy drugs and realize a profit if he sold them for $400. Some guys put him up to it, but James learned that they were were planning to rob and kill him as soon as he collected. He found this out at some wild, drug/drinking party. He promptly fled to his home in Beaver Dam. He never did collect.

"Seven years he has spent in prison," says Ambrose, "and he still hasn't learned his lesson." He shakes his head: "Seven years — not all at once, but added up. All that time he spent here, then he goes and does a thing like that!"

"No." he says, and shakes his head.

†††

August 15, 1989—
Sign by Matthew on the mop handle in the lavatory:
Who borrows returns;
Who wets wrings.
Another one:
The freight elevator has an open grate and a sign on the shaft wall floats by: *Live and Let Live.*

†††

One that Father Peter (Aikens) had inscribed under the visor he wore in choir:
God Alone.

✝✝✝

April 6, 1991—

For his introduction at Mass Father Alan said: "Prayer that is bad is like bad weather: It is better than no weather at all."

✝✝✝

July 14, 1991—

I asked Brother Victor why we never have forest fires here the way we used to. It was a regular thing back in the 1950s. He said we had them then because the brothers used to go out and set those fires.

"Why?" I said.

"Well, the choir monks were in charge of fire fighting, and the novices and young ones especially found it an exciting break in a dull routine. So we would provide them with some excitement.

"There was a rule in the old usages that every year the Abbot in Chapter performed a rite of excommunication for any arsonists. We would be down at the other end of the Chapter laughing up our sleeves."

I myself remember the last time the ceremony was performed, before the custom was discontinued. In full regalia, with crozier in one hand and a lighted candle in the other, the Abbot pronounced excommunication on any arsonists, and threw the lighted candle on the floor. Poor Dom James hated doing this, and was nearly in tears.

I wondered what an irony it would be should the candle set the wooden floor afire.

✝✝✝

The young monks were not the only ones to get excited about forest fires. Father Louis Merton was the forester, and would approach a burning site with great energy. His enthusiasm was infectious, especially to novices like me. Upon coming to my first grass fire I grabbed a broom, began beating it soundly, only to cause it to spread in all directions.

This was due return for the smugness I felt from the previous fire, one that was in a wooded area. We had driven to a valley, and after a short walk Father Louis spotted smoke down the valley where it was densely accumulated. I headed up the hill realizing the smoke was drifting from that direction, found the fire and was fighting it an hour before Father Louis arrived.

By the time the fire was under control it was dark, and our

crew headed towards the highway to phone the monastery for a ride home. We found a Pepsi store, and gathered in a circle enjoying a conversation that must have perplexed the country man behind the counter.

Someone noticed the clock was stopped shortly before seven o'clock, although it was much later. The clerk said it has been that way for years and he never intends to fix it. The kids have to go home after seven, so in his store it is always before seven.

†††

Tree planting was another favorite enthusiasm for Father Louis. One spring we took a batch of seedlings to the woods. He wanted to transplant a young dogwood from the woods for the garden near the novitiate, so before leaving the garden I dug a hole. When we arrived in the forest and located a suitable young sapling, we dug it up by the roots and wrapped it in burlap. He meant to leave it there until the end of work time, but I suggested it would get too dry. Father Louis told me to carry it back now. And run. It was a mile and although the ball was heavy I ran the whole way and planted it immediately. By the time I had finished and was scraping mud off my boots Father Louis arrived and remarked: "Spring is the sport of monks."

†††

Beards were permitted for lay brothers only until early in the sixties when many things began to change. I was one of the first wave of Choir-monks to grow a beard. Father Louis was not too enthusiastic about the results. I learned yesterday, from a former novice, he complained about me, with my baby face, and this huge beard: "It's not right!"

Father Louis was himself well endowed with bushy eyebrows. During spiritual direction he sat with his back to the window, and the novice in front would see little more than a silhouette with overhanging eyebrows attached. This was temporarily changed once when the Undermaster, Father Tarcisius, shaved them off during hair cutting. It made Father Louis look a little too benign, and he would, in certain moods, assume the deportment of an Oxford Don and remark on this or that as: "Most extraordinary!" or "Most edifying!"

This was almost an imitation, but not quite: He was showing a streak of something in himself.

✝✝✝

December 1, 1991—

The farm boss, Brother Conrad, read aloud from the Book of Revelations at Mass: "I am the Alfalfa and Omega."

One of the novices keeps reading King Nebuchadnezzar as "King Ne-bucket-dinosaur."

✝✝✝

December 4, 1991—

A note on the bulletin board, directed to someone's excessive generosity in giving away community property:

Someone borrowed my personal mug in the refectory. I hope, whoever it is given to appreciate it as much as I did when it was first given to me by a friend.

If you need anything else, please feel free to visit my room on Tuesday or Thursday. I'm usually gone between 8:30 and 3 p.m. If what is exposed doesn't appeal to you, look under my desk.

✝✝✝

November 5, 1993—

Ambrose saw a dove acting funny, flopping around, hardly able to fly. He caught it and saw its gullet was swollen. Opening its beak he saw a grain of corn caught inside, swollen up in the throat. He picked it out. The dove shook its head and flew off.

Similar to a story Brother Guerric Plante told. He was sitting outside in meditation, with his back to a large pane window, hands resting open in his lap. A hummingbird flew into the window, bounced and landed in his open hands. Both remained immobile, one man of enormous girth and one tiny bird. Guerric waited, breathless, until the bird stirred, recovered, shook its head, perched on his finger and flew away.

Eventually, that became an enchanted spot. Guerric fed regular visitors there: A wounded fox, a raccoon, a skunk, two field cats. Sometimes all appeared on the same evening.

✝✝✝

August 29, 1994—

I was awakened from my mid-day nap by a helicopter flying over and circling around repeatedly and not moving on. I looked out the window and a clutch of monks had already gathered to watch its maneuvers. It circled low over the woods

36

just north of us, then crossed the highway and landed in a field. I decided to chase it down, but before I got there it took off and returned to the wooded area again, up the slope. It landed again, and this time, determined, I hurried up through the thicket of briars and came out on the open field where they were parked. There were about four men inside and I was going to approach when one held up his hand to stop me. He crossed the field, opened a wallet from his shirt pocket: Nelson County Police. I did not say what I wanted to say: "Please! you are interrupting my siesta!" What I said is: "Well, now that you have caused all this excitement, what is it all about?" He said: "We found ninety marijuana plants in those woods."

They were hanging out of the door of the helicopter, lush and richly green. What is so astonishing, is how close it was, not a three-minute walk from the main building. Later, three of us go to find the patch. It was well hidden in a covert no one ever visits. Except the anonymous monk who reported the find.

✝✝✝

March 23, 1995—

Some monks live a charmed life. Giles, age 87, was returning from a cataract operation in the pick-up, driven by Brother Ephrem, 78, our retired Cellarer. The road was narrow with poor shoulders, they went off and the truck landed upside down. Both were unhurt. Giles, still in his seat belt, suspended up side down like a bat by his seat belt, turned to his companion and said: "Gee, the eye Doctor said I am not even supposed to bend over." Ephrem meanwhile was vexed because his papers were all scattered.

Cars stopped, got them out, and shoved the truck back on its wheels, still in good operating condition, and the two drove off, none the worse. The eye healed properly.

✝✝✝

July 8, 1995—

Brother Victor died of cancer, after about a year of retirement from cheese production. It became increasingly obvious that he was making too many mistakes with the cheese. He was diagnosed with Alzheimer's disease, and in his most jovial manner he would always approach me with the same observation: "You know there is one thing I can't get over about you... Your beard is grey and when you came to the monastery your hair was all black."

With Victor's death the monastery loses one of its most fluent storytellers. By now, of course, everyone has heard enough of World War II in the Pacific, and how it ended when his ship got there.

✝✝✝

July 12, 1995—

Brother Guerric had a dream about Victor. He saw his grave, and over it was a great fiery column. Its energy seemed to surge upward, and open out at the top. There emerged shining letters: VICTOR VICTORIOUS. He was given to understand that this is Victor's title. Whenever there is some calamity or disaster, Victor will be there to help anyone who calls on him.

✝✝✝

December 12, 1995—

Brother Giles, the bookbinder, does fine watercolors, and in his 80s continues to experiment with new approaches, new to him, both in abstract and realist styles. I was impressed by a grey-blue abstract, muted tones, serene and spontaneous, with some hint of a boat. He considered it "a piece of cheese," and made hints at tearing it up. I entered the book bindery when I knew he was present, grabbed it, and headed for the door, concealing none of my actions. When I reached the door he said: "Give that to me." I said: "No, I want it." He came over, and since he is short I held it higher than his reach. "Give it here." I protested it is an image of the sacred and is blasphemy to tear up. He wouldn't accept that, so what can you do? I gave it to him. I watched him tear it in four pieces and thrust it into the trash barrel. Then he thanked me for co-operating. Maybe I should have taken it when he was absent. But then, I did not think it right.

✝✝✝

January 16, 1996—

The new choir director moved the Abbot from the choir stall where the light panel, with its dozens of switches, could be controlled. It did not seem suitable that the Abbot should be invested with such a chore. The Abbot had different ideas: "They took away the last bit of control I had."

✝✝✝

February 4, 1996—

Brother Guerric, whose room is next to Giles, became concerned when on several successive nights he heard a thump against the wall, usually after bed time. Since Giles is 85 he asked if he were having fainting spells.

"No, I am in bed reading, and if I don't like the book I throw it against the wall."

"Well," says Guerric, "would you kindly find another wall throw it against, you're waking me up."

†††

February 8, 1996—

The phone had rung for about the sixth time this morning with a call for Ambrose. Not surprising. Usually it is some unfortunate needing wood for the fireplace, or some advice. Before handing him the phone I asked if he wanted me to tell the caller he was not in. He said no.

After talking for ten minutes Ambrose hung up, and said he was sorry he took that phone call. Norma Jean needed a ride to the courthouse, which might end in being a ride to jail. She had called three times already. She had no transportation — she had wrecked her car, and had no insurance. Since this is required in Kentucky, she had to appear in court. If justice takes its course, her two children will be left at home without a mother. And without a father, since he had departed — not Claude, long since departed — but David, a younger and more recent man who also once had a job here thanks to Ambrose.

†††

February 9, 1995—

With assistance from Brother Frederic the bookkeeper, Norma Jean was able to return home. Next day a call came for firewood. She had been heating the house by turning up the oven. There was no way for her to get wood since the steering wheel on the car was bent out of shape.

Days later, I noticed the huge supply of firewood stacked by the hermitage had diminished to almost nothing!

†††

August 3, 1996—

Things are quite tame now in the monastery compared to when we aspired to a severe ideal of strictness as in the 1950s. Strictness seemed to inspire its opposite. I recall the time I was meditating in Church, while on the opposite side of the church Brother Tobias was quietly making his confession to Father Lambert. Our confessionals were simple open kneelers with no walls.

Father Lambert had recently preached a sermon in which he complained: "Why is it no one in our monasteries ever has a vision of the Blessed Mother?" — as though it indicated a lack of fervor.

As I was pondering on a line from the Magnificat, I was distracted by a sudden figure of a woman, wrapped in many colored scarves, walking from behind the altar past the confessional, towards the sacristy door: Short, quiet and swift.

It was a shock to see a woman in the front of the church, which was strictly part of the enclosure area, a woman who looked small and Mediterranean. When she was gone there was a disturbance at the confessional. I got up and crossed over as the two of them came in my direction. Brother Tobias said radiantly: "Did you see her?" And I said, yes.

"Where did she go?"

We tried the sacristy door, but it was locked, so obviously she couldn't have gone there and must have disappeared.

When I told all this to the Undermaster of Novices, Father Tarcisius, I explained the mysterious disappearance because the sacristy was locked. At that something clicked in his mind.

He said the door locks from the inside, and during the day it is always left unlocked.

He said the apparition was Brother Iranaeus, a short, dark complexioned man, who works in the tailor shop where fabrics of all colors are available.

Ten years later I was assigned to help Tobias in the Retreathouse making beds. One day he asked: "Have you ever seen Our Lady?"

I had forgotten that episode and said no.

Ten years after that conversation I had remembered it again, brought up the question and asked if he had ever seen Mary. He hesitated a long time, dredging something up from the murky bottoms. Finally he muttered something about people making exaggerations.

This was towards the end of his life.

Communications are very slow in the monastery.

Conversation between three monks in the kitchen:

"Is there singing in heaven?" says the plumber, a black monk who came searching for his flashlight.

"We will all sing Bach without knowing music." replies the cook.

"It will be unlike anything we know." the short elder says.

"All music will be one note." says the plumber with flash in hand. "In this life we never quite get the pitch; not until you get there will you hear the pitch."

The senior retorts: "That's something for this life. There, everyone will sing whatever they want and it will sound all right."

Conclusion

On December 8, 1997, the feast of the Immaculate Conception, when the planet Venus was in conjunction with the crescent moon, Brother Guerric died of an aneurysm in the lungs. With him goes a reliable source of information about the history of the monastery since the '50s, many memories, stories and vivid imitations of characters in and around the monastery.

John Joseph Fagenbush lives a free life, sort of like a street monk. He takes part time jobs and works in soup kitchens, sleeps in a tent and travels about the country from one work pool to another. Last time I saw him he was cooling his feet in a public fountain in Louisville talking to an old man.

Jeff Fagenbush acquired a degree in electrical engineering in Texas, married and has two children. He works for a trucking firm in Colorado.

Brother Ambrose still works in the kitchen, but less frequently now, thanks to a relative temporarily employed in his place. He has slowed down but may in fact never die, and it is a mystery to the kitchen crew where he spends his time. Perhaps he is in solitude at the hermitage, or fixing it up, or fixing houses for poor neighbors, or maybe the hermitage is for one of the black, Mexican or a recovering drug addict, or he is getting a kid out of jail for stealing a car, or...

Part Two

Sign Language

Brother Guerric Plante

SIGN LANGUAGE

The train from Louisville arrived at Gethsemane Station on time Thursday morning, December 29, 1952. Brother Hugh was waiting by the side of a new GMC dump truck. He loaded up the mail sack in back and the passenger in front. Our conversation during the one mile ride to the monastery consisted of two words:

"Retreat?"

"Yes."

Father Francis, the guestmaster, was on hand to greet me. We went up the main front stairs in the monastery building to the third floor. He showed me to a large room with old fashioned mismatched furniture, with a cotton mattress on the bed.

"Are you here to stay?" he asked.

"No, Father. I'm here during the school Christmas break, I will be here for three days."

He bowed and retreated, saying:

"Stay as long as you wish."

A few days later, after an interview with the Novice Master and Father Abbot, I was admitted to the lay-brother novitiate.

It was a custom in the goods old days of monastic life to provide a "guardian angel," instructor monk, for each layman when he began religious life as a postulant. The new way of life was explained in silence, using sign language. Two weeks were allowed to learn liturgical and house rules. Most important was a beginner's knowledge of sign language.

All of the above was done in silence. First step: Mimic the guardian angel and others. Second step: Try to remember. Third step: Practice what you learn. The second week became easier when I learned some basic signs — eat, sleep, pray, work.

Time: Hold closed fists together, extend little fingers.
Hot: Open mouth and heat your palm with breath.
Cold: Make shivering motions with hands.
Think: Point forefinger to the head.
Hear: Cup hand behind the ear.
Red: Pull lower lip forward.

This was great, but my learning was not fast enough for seventeen year old Brother Adrian, otherwise known as my "angel guardian." He signed to me "Hurry up!" and wrote it our for this big, slow twenty year old layman. Brother Adrian signed:

"Follow me."

We went single file to the cemetery. On the way I learned "cross": Forefingers crossed. Many crosses equal "cemetery."

We arrived at the cemetery wall. Brother Adrian signed: "Bow your head" — we are going to pray, I thought.

A sudden gentle, but firm shove from Brother Adrian knocked my head into the cemetery wall. Hurriedly straightening up, I fixed my eyes on the stern young man while tightening my fists for a different kind of sign language.

Brother Adrian was rapping the middle knuckle of his right hand on the back of his left hand. Somehow I knew this meant "Hard." When he pointed to my head, what else could it mean?

From that point on it became easy.

Gravel on the ground: Sign "hard," sign "little" (rubbing thumb with forefinger.)
Brick: Draw rectangle, sign "red," sign "hard."
Pointing to himself: "Tough cookie."

What a wonder! I suddenly seemed to catch on and needed no more instruction. What an awakening! A new language that named people and things!

Machine: Rotate thumbs over each other.
Garden: Sign "vegetable" (close finger of right hand and make motion of planting.)
Tractor: Sign "garden — machine."
Train: Sign "horse — machine."
Egbert: Sign "egg — bird."

Sugar

The elder Brother Albert was instructing me in traditional ways of preparing the garden. I was still newly arrived in the community and was being as patient as I could.

I was a beautiful spring day. The sun and its warmth made the green thumbs tingle on each of us. The energy in the air stimulated our imaginations to visualize rows of cabbage, tomatoes, sweet potatoes; all of the hundreds of plants that one day would give their energy, in turn, to the prayer life of the monks.

While Brother Albert remembered the good old ways of farming, and since I had been to agricultural school, I has some doubt about the instructions I was receiving about old world farming:

"So you see, mine brudder, you must have horse manure when it has passed the heat of fermentation. Never the new green stuff, too hot! Too much energy, to quick, very bad, always you must be obedient to God's will, the law of nature. You see that is what makes the monk different. He learns the right way and sticks to it."

I was full of the latest, modern ways of agriculture of the 1950's: Chemical fertilizer, pest control, etc. I wanted to explain it all and was thinking fast.

"I see you do not like the old ways, mine young brudder, so I will tell you a true story that happened to me and so I am convinced of the right way of obedience."

"Several years go mine Abbot gave me the responsibility as interior Cellerar to manage the supplies needed to feed the community and guest. This was a job of overseeing supplies for the storeroom, supervision of the cooks and menu as well as keeping the wine cellar. When I told mine Abbot: "This is too mush for a little old brother like me." he said: "Brother Albert do what is necessary to keep the peace. I don't want anyone upset."

"And so, Brother Guerric, I organized the work as best could. Saturdays — orders for next week delivery. Wednesdays — delivery of all supplies. Storeroom open one hour. No extras. No substitutes. Report all to the Abbot.

"The cook for the guests came to me on a Monday, an Irishman named Finbar The supply of sugar had run out, and he demanded sugar: '...now or the apples will spoil if I don't use them. Think of poverty, brother!' he said.

"But I had no sugar, so I said: 'Will speak to the Abbot about this.'

"The Abbot said: 'Brother Albert, give the sugar.'

So Brother Albert told me how he went to the storeroom and knelt next to the empty sugar barrel. He prayed to Our Lady for help. Then he lifted the lid to peer over the edge of the tall barrel, and the light from the bulb in the ceiling shined on sugar crystal lining the inside barrel wall. So with a spoon he scraped and scraped until the wood of the barrel was clean.

Brother got up, reminded himself of humility by placing a finger on the tip of his nose, pushing it down. Then carrying the package of sugar under his arm, Brother Albert presented the gift to Brother Finbar with a little bow and went to church for Vespers.

Later, after prayers, Father Abbot called Brother to his office to thank him for restoring peace and to make sure a lesson was learned.

When Brother Albert ended this long instruction for me in the garden, he looked at me in silence for a long time, then said: 'You understand the lesson I learned the hard way, do you? I tell this story to you — so young — to keep and practice all your life.

"Remember this as the sweetness of your monastic life."

Jerusalem Bread

There was a little more activity than usual in the monastery bakery that Thursday morning. The chief cook sent word from the kitchen to replace the bread supply with fresh bread before the noon meal.

"Both types," he said. "Whole wheat and white."

However, the usual daily quota of fruit cakes to fill the Abbey's customer orders could not take second place. What could we do?

The bakery crew of four monks handled the situation easily.

"Haven't we worked together for over a year?" asked the boss. "Now is the time to show our expertise and efficiency. "Brother Joel, measure the flour!"

"Brother Guerric, prepare the sugar, salt and oleo. Don't forget the powdered milk, then you can help me with the fruit cake while the brothers do the bread mix. I will mix the yeast when the time calls for it. Someone put the covers over the mixing bowls until I am ready."

Two hours later, when the fruit cakes were finished to perfection, Brother Joel adjusted the oven temperature to 400 degrees. By now the bread dough is mixed and ready for the baking pans. Eighty loaves of coarse whole wheat, eighty loaves of light white bread.

The bread was in the oven for 15 minutes before anyone realized something was wrong. The bread was flat in the pans. Each loaf remained the size of a brick. The white bread was normal, but the wheat bread was ruined — or was it?

The four bakers reluctantly admitted failure and removed the bricks from the oven. One said: "It is not too late. Let's use some advertisement skills on the bread. If we only think of a name or a slogan we can sell this bread that looks like nice building blocks."

Father John popped up with a Scriptural quotation: "Let's call it Jerusalem Bread, because 'Jerusalem is built like a city, strongly compact' — psalm 121!"

So with pieces of brown wrapping paper, tape, magic marker and many prayers later, signs had been constructed saying:

"Jerusalem Bread, New Recipe"

"One turn Only"

"Try it, you'll like it"

"Healthy High Fiber Bread"

"Limited Supply - All natural ingredients"

"New Taste Treat"

The above were all placed in the food service area on time for the noon meal.

The sales program really worked. Twenty loaves of bread had been eaten by the end of the day, along with the meal of pasta, vegetables, soup and cheese.

No one knew until later what really happened. For there had been so much rushing around and so many adjustments to be made that only yeast, flour and water were mixed for the bread. All of the other ingredients had been forgotten.

When this was discovered, there was a minor rebellion in the cloister until the four bakers were obliged to kneel before the community and confess the mistake and apologize for disrupting the orderly atmosphere by such worldly ways of advertising.

When peace was restored the youngest in the group, a novice, said dryly: "Now we should call them Loaves of Love."

Ecstasy/Agony

The approach to Thomas Merton's hermitage seems different each time I visit the cement block cabin. This must be because nature is either in a riot or very quiet when I make my visit. My visits have been in either May or October for a retreat week.

It is now the middle of May, and I am beginning the seven day retreat in solitude. I recall the January day when Father Abbot said to me: "Yes I think it would be good for you to make a private retreat. How about May 12th?"

"Yes, I said, spring time is the best time to make a retreat in the woods, close to nature. The cabin will be cool at night and a fire might be needed on a rainy day. Thank you.

Everywhere I look I find a touch of spring as I walk along the rough roadway toward the hermitage. To the left is the pink dogwood tree. To the right of the porch is a large red bud tree. Close to the porch foundation is a planting of day lilies already in bud. Overhead are locust, oak, pine, juniper and black walnut trees. Weaving through the branches are some of the local birds, finches, a few humming birds, many cardinals, blue jays and a crow doing sentry duty.

I arrive at the cinder block building with enough food for the week and a change of clothing; a few books on prayer and a novel by Stephen King, several cans of soup, some bread and cheese, fresh fruit and several types of dry beans, some onions and of course rice.

Settling in is simple. Books go in the wide front room at the table facing the window. Clothing and sheets into the bedroom behind the kitchen, and food is placed in the cupboard and refrigerator in the kitchen. I visit the chapel and already the afternoon sun is changing to a rosy glow among the clouds.

Is rain coming? — better to walk in the woods later this evening. I'll listen to the Poor-will, and get not much sleep tonight.

No mosquitoes.

Monday:

Visited the woodshed this morning to bring the mower out to the front yard. I saluted the large snake draped over the inside of the door frame.

Scared Mamma Ground Hog from under the shed with her two little ones.

The birds are asking for bread crumbs. Why wouldn't they eat the dry cereal?

Tuesday:

Rain today. No mowing. Temperature 45 and going up.

Already Wednesday — time flies.

I did not read much of the Stephen King novel.

Pray. Mow. Pick up dead branches. Prepare soup, grilled cheese sandwiches. Wash a T-shirt. Hang it on a hanger on a nail outside on the porch.

Did Merton leave anything on his book shelf? Here is an original Monastic Exchange consisting of essays from the monks of various monasteries in the United States about proposed changes in the monastic life style. Ho Hum! All of that is history.

Is there anything else? Monks Pond was an original literary quarterly edited by Father Louis and printed by the print shop Brothers. While paging through the articles, poetry and artwork I recall seeing Merton at the collating table in the printery. He used to grab the printed sheets as they revolved in front of him on the table. Hopefully each page would be in numerical sequence and right side up. It was manual work he enjoyed doing for his friends.

I closed my eyes while recalling the past and was enjoying the smell of the wood pile, stove ashes, fresh pine and juniper. Suddenly the rocking chair twitched and vibrated. Chattering came from the blinds on the windows. The air cooled. The T-shirt began to sway on its hanger.

Out doors there was no breeze. The venetian blinds were still, and I was more quiet then usual with wonder.

No lights tonight. Forget the fresh bean soup! In the chapel I pray - one candle.

What happened? There is no one here with whom to share the experience.

Finally to bed. Awake...

Thursday:

Light sleep. Early to rise. Prayer in the chapel - both candles. Coffee gets cold while meditating on the events of yesterday.

The horizon looks the same. The sun is in its usual place. No trees have fallen.

Keep busy. Prepare to leave.

Where is Brother Harold when I need him? He will not arrive for my return to the monastery until Sunday morning.

Until then... sweep, scrub, dust, mop the floor. Make a stew of the leftovers.

What was it? Wind of Spirit? A Merton practical joke? Too much solitude!

No message yet.

Sunday morning coffee:

Prepare breakfast for two. Toast and Jelly, scrambled eggs. Where is Brother Harold? It's eight o'clock. No sound on the road. Did he have a flat tire?

At last at 8:25 I hear a scrunch on the gravel road... hurry up and park the pick up truck!

"Brother Harold!" — he is out of the truck. NOW.

"Brother Harold I have something important to say to you!"

"Forget it," said Harold, "I have something more important to tell you so listen to me first."

I said, "No, you don't understand."

"Yes I do, " he said. "You can wait. Didn't you practice patience at all during this past week? You would not know it maybe, but our part of Kentucky had an earthquake. Very few of the monks noticed it. I was in my room on the second floor and the door closed all by itself. Isn't that something? I also heard something fall on the floor next door. One of the priests in the sacristy thought he heard the bells start to ring. Did you hear the bells? Was there anything you noticed. It happened Thursday afternoon about 4:30. Were you here? Do you recall anything unusual?

"Go ahead. it's your turn. What was it that was so impor-tant?"

Patience.

Feet in the Air

"Reverend Father," said the voice on the Abbot's phone, "I had to call you this early in the morning because I just found him."

"Brother Wilfred are you in the infirmary doing your work?" asked the Abbot. "Whom did you find? Where?"

"Well, Reverend Father," continued Brother Wilfred, I looked into the room... you know, in the infirmary... where he's been. Oh! it was awful. He's on the floor!"

"Which room?" asked the Abbot. "Is it Brother John? He is 96 after all... is it Brother Boniface with his broken hip? Did Father Augustine try to get out of bed without his wooden leg? Please give me a name, Willie!"

"Well, you see, I was a little late covering for him last night," he gasped, "because I said an extra rosary for all the sick and you are included in my morning prayer for all the trouble I am causing, but you told me to report anything as soon as it happened. I didn't have my glasses with me the first time and the whole room was fuzzy. My hearing is still good and I could tell he wasn't moving around as he usually does when he hears me coming down the hall. I try to be as quiet as I can, you know, but I had been a nurse with the Alexian Brothers for so long that it's a little hard sometimes - no I did not whisper or sing, even I know it's the Great Silence time of the night. Like that time I did an x-ray — did I tell you...?"

"No, Brother Wilfred, not now!" interrupted the Abbot.

"Oh yes, thank you for the reminder," he said, taking a deep breath, "I was going to tell you — he was laying on his back with his feet in the air. He meant a lot to me and I took such good care of him. I don't know if you remember his name since you only saw him once. He was a gift, you see. Yes, that's the one Reverend Father, Pretty Boy was his name.

"What should I do with him? Well, if you don't mind - just so it isn't against obedience, that is — I have him wrapped in tissue paper in a large match box and I am calling to ask permission to bury my parakeet in the cemetery.

"—Father Abbot are you still there? What was that last comment about doing penance? What did I do now!"

PART THREE

ORDINARY ICONS

FATHER TIMOTHY KELLY

FATHER ROGER RENO

The passage in the second reading (Job 17:1, 23-27) says that "the whole creation has been groaning in travail together until now; and not only creation, but we ourselves, who have the first fruits of the Spirit groan inwardly as we wait for adoption as sons, the redemption of our bodies." This passage sums up what was probably Father Roger's basic stance before the Almighty. Certainly the word groaning characterizes his manner of speaking and tone of voice; but more so, the reality that he truly longed for eternal life. In fact, as he told most of us, "I am eager for eternity."

To be eager for eternity must also show in one's life.

This was the case with Father Roger.

His life was marked by a real fidelity to those many things that comprise the monastic life. The office with his Brothers was essential for him. For several months, he expressed concern because his health did not always allow him to be present. The Mass was central in his day, and as he had been one who preached the idea of the monk as a victim soul, he viewed daily Eucharist as a true identification with the one victim who saves us all, and the source of strength to share in the redemptive mission of Christ. Even up to the end he was faithful at least to a gesture of manual labor.

Though it was not immediately obvious, Father had a real sense of humor which not only saw behind much that happens in community living, but also was able to make a comment that would create a climate of truth. He always loved Bishop Sheen's story — in fact he was almost sure it was divinely inspired — the fact that God created zebras and giraffes was a true sign of God's sense of humor.

His eagerness for eternity never separated him from a concern about "what's new." One is reminded of the Desert Father story of the travelers who went to the wilds of the desert to seek out a certain Father for a word of salvation. Finally, upon reaching him they were astounded that his first question was: "How goes the world?" Father Roger was no world hater and though his concern was generally about the dark side of things, he always could profess his faith that all things would be fulfilled in eternity.

Father's concern for life, his humor, his continued life of faithfulness were hard won. His health had been a burden for him for many years. In the years after his ordination he served the community as Master of the Brothers, and was a regular confessor to the novices. His conferences and his direction always had elements of humor, and were an expression of the classical spiritual doctrine of those days that he made a very real part of his life. But the heart condition made it necessary for him to cease this role.

In addition to his physical difficulties, he suffered greatly from scruples and a sense of insecurity which was not that obvious to most, but was a constant burden all his life. He had true docility and humility. Though I was many years his junior, he would, with great openness, present his personal struggles to me and heed whatever comment was given. He realized the burden it could be for those who were asked to share his difficulties, So he would endeavor not to be a burden. Once he had given his confidence to a fellow monk, he would stand by it no matter how difficult.

Although few of us really knew Father Roger, all did have some relation with him. Undoubtedly his council to each of us now would be the same as was reflected in his life during these last several months especially — *to be eager for eternity.* To be eager for eternity as was he, by doing the works of faith. In the works of faith the spirit of the Lord lives and groans that most perfect prayer.

—7 DEC 1977

It would have been very interesting to hear the discussion between the Angel of Death and Brother Ferdinand. Undoubtedly, when Brother was told that his going forth would be one with the liturgical celebration of the death of the Lord, he probably shook his head vigorously, put out his jaw and said: "No, that would cause the brothers too much trouble, and I don't want to be a burden to the Brothers. They got enough already, just putting up with the likes of me."

But then a day or so later, Brother Ferdinand would have meekly appeared before the Angel and said: "Say, what we were talking about the other day, you know, dying during the "sacred triduum," well if you think that's what should be done, it's OK with me. I just haven't had any peace since saying 'No.' It is just my pride and self will. Something just said to me 'Old man, you just be quiet and obey.' I just didn't want to give nobody a hard time!"

And so his heavy breathing slowed and his countenance relaxed, and today he is with his Lord.

All of us knew Brother Ferdinand. He had a very specific and personal relationship with each of us. He could tell when one of us was having a hard time, and he'd pray a little special for that Brother. Probably watch him over the top of his glasses as he looked up from praying the Psalms. He loved the psalms so much it was almost a necessity for us to commend him to the Lord during this time when we would be praying the psalms at length.

During the last couple of years, try as he might, he had been unable to read any book except for the Psalter. But the Lord even seemed to question that. Brother Ferdinand expressed his concern when in the Louisville hospital that it was nothing but pride that would have the likes of him praying psalms. That was for good monks. He should return to praying the rosary. But then maybe the rosary would cause the man in the next bed to be upset: "So what to do Father? I am confused."

This was something he experienced, just being confused: "Don't know just what to do," he would say. But this confusion, according to Brother Ferdinand, was caused by one thing: Not accepting the Cross; not being abandoned.

"Just abandon yourself to the Cross, that's all you have to do, because the Cross will always be there."

And it was always there in Brother's life.

Brother Ferdinand came to the monastery in his forties, after running the family bakery for years. Although somewhat successful at it, that was "just too much trying to keep everybody at peace."

In the list of those whom he remembered by name each morning at Mass was his chief competition in the bakery business. Even the baker he had to fire because he drank a little too much, a little too often.

Life hadn't been real easy before the bakery. There were the farms during the Depression. But to him, everyone always had it more difficult than he did. For Brother Ferdinand, his whole life had been a struggle to see how to help someone: In the Legion of Mary, in the local service clubs, or feeding the calves when other brothers had more important things to do.

Life in the monastery hadn't been that easy either.

Brother had a bad stomach — but he didn't want to cause anybody any trouble. He had something of a nervous breakdown. It can be said he, like the patriarch Jacob, wrestled with the angel until he received a blessing. Brother Ferdinand wrestled with the Lord, and though, like Jacob, scarred by the struggle, he won.

In the last few years with the many changes in our way of life, Brother often had the joy of sharing his exuberance for the spiritual life with his brothers. He'd recommend books to them, but always in a subtle way since he didn't want to bother anyone. He'd also recommend tapes, and often would share words of encouragement with his fellow monks.

And the encouragement he received from his fellow brothers was always a special grace for Brother Ferdinand, something for which he could never express sufficient gratitude.

These included the encouragement from the brothers with whom he had worked for many years and from whom he received moral support in the midst of his nervous difficult; a Brother who each day made a few hand signs to him; the old brothers who were so capable in every way, and "put up with the likes of me," as he would say.

These relationships, along with the simple joy of the calves running to him as he approached, were the sacraments of God's love that added joy to his daily life.

One can't help but look on the strong, noble, peaceful face of Brother and be reminded of an old desert Father, a St. Anthony, or St. Benedict. We know in the life of Anthony, that after years of a struggle that had left its scars, he was this serene, gentle person with a certain wholeness in every way that attracted young disciples. St. Benedict, who, after the early years of solitary struggle, was the gathering point for many disciples, and who, as death approached, saw the whole of the world gathered into a single ray of light.

And so this morning, my brothers, as we stand in the light of the Cross we know something of its victory, not just in its own historical moment, but in the life of our Brother Ferdinand who saw everything in the light of the Cross. He was marked by the sign of the Cross and knew there was and is no other way. His word of encouragement to each of us would be to accept the Cross, abandon ourselves to it — because it is the reality of life and it will always be there.

We probably wince at the message — it's not popular in the newest psycho-socio terms, but the terrible reality is that it has worked. The Gospel criteria is too well established — "by their fruits you will know them."

And like the one who hung beside Jesus and asked only to be remembered in his kingly power, not asking to be freed from the cross, so Brother Ferdinand never asked to be freed from his cross, only to live it till the end. Today he is in Paradise; today he is with his God, the former things have passed away. He waited for his God and he can now be glad and rejoice in his salvation.

—24 MARCH 1978 (GOOD FRIDAY)

It is not the powerful, the rich, the successful ones who are God's life in the here and now; it is rather the poor, the gentle, those who suffer, who know how to be merciful, those who are single hearted and lovers of peace.

Perhaps this element from the beatitudes, or happiness, was something that we most easily connect with Brother Zachary.

Basically he was a happy person — he loved life and lived it fully on many levels and never from a purely selfish optic.

But it wasn't because his experience of life was without complication, At a very young age he suffered from physical disorders which later complicated his vision and his hearing. However, this in no way deterred his ever growing interests, his desire to learn, his wish to be of service to others and never to burden anyone. Anything he had, any talent he possessed was always for others, so much so that he experienced certain frustration at being incapable of serving as much as he desired.

Brother Zachary's work assignment at the Gatehouse in the days when it was a religious articles store brought him into contact with very many visitors. He was always most congenial, remembered people, showed concern for them, and willingly shared his own spiritual evolution with others to encourage them in the ways of the Lord. When the assignment was complete Brother rejoiced to be totally within the community, and though many continued to ask for him, his response was to keep them very particularly in his prayers.

For this he had to be most faithful to the monastic solitude he had originally chosen.

As Christian monks we are being called ever anew into the life of the Spirit, the life of conversion in the fullness of beatitude. This was a very real element constantly present in our Brother Zachary, and his monastic profession was a culminating witness to his desire to be totally one with Jesus. There was the restlessness that St. Augustine had proclaimed that could only find its peace, its beatitude when resting in the Lord. That was part of Brother Zachary's life.

Brother Zachary came into the Catholic Church from another Christian denomination. Within the Church he then sought to give himself ever more completely, first as an Alexian Brother working with the sick, then to our own monastic community in order to be more closely united to the life of the Lord Jesus. His was one of those very particular vocations. He never once doubted his call to Gethsemani.

His generous response was often spoken amidst the pain and anguish of these last weeks, wanting to know in what way he had not given enough; or how he could give more.

The Infirmarian could respond that all that was necessary was to drink the grape juice!! He wanted only to give himself entirely for the Lord. And the Lord had taken his generous, sensitive heart seriously, as he had to depend more and more on others and suffer many inconveniences from his sickness.

Now his response to God's call, his desire for happiness is filled, now his growth, his spiritual evolution has come to a whole new plateau. He knew that God who wanted to share his happiness with his people; he knew the Lord Jesus by sharing in the life of pain and death that won for us eternal joy. Only a Brother Zachary who was set on the mind and heart of Christ can know the true meaning of beatitude. The happiness that can fill a purified and unselfish heart, the Beatitude that is pure gift because it is the life of God.

—25 August 1978

The Gospel we have just heard (John 11:17-27), is obviously chosen for its strong affirmation of Resurrection and eternal life for all who believe. In this context, an affirmation of our Brother Pachomius' going forth into the life he professed in his faith and exemplified in his daily living.

But the Gospel can also be construed to fit the liturgical day we celebrate — the feast of the Holy Family — though Martha, Mary, and Lazarus are not the commonly referred to Holy Family, nevertheless families exhibit the care, concern, and dedication to life, to each other, that families are meant to foster and which the unique Holy Family exemplifies.

This reminds of Brother Pachomius. We always appreciated his generous hospitality, the real personal concern he always shared with our own families when they visited the monastery. T

he Christian welcome, and unselfish service that the Rule of St. Benedict says should characterize the monk's response to the guest, who in a special way is Christ in our midst, was the example Brother Pachomius always presented. T

he hour of arrival, the type of persons, their needs, no matter what, always provoked a response of equanimity, of generosity, of human gentleness.

Family was something at the core of Brother's vocation. Not surprising, since his first choice in life had been marriage. But in the mysterious ways of God it was not to be fruitful or lasting.

To continue in his life of dedication where God could be all and no self-centered interest distract him from the radical demands of Christian commitment, Brother entered the monastery, and took upon himself all the ways that monastic life offers to totally dedicate oneself to God.

Brother was not only interested in his service to the guests, but in all living things — flowers, birds, dogs. And all brought forth his gentle care. His biggest concern was for the life of the community and each and every Brother.

In the terms of common parlance he was an affirming person who encouraged a Brother in his projects, be they little or great. He not only noticed, but was genuinely interested in each Brother's life as a monk and would express sorrow at someone who seemed to ignore the means that the monastic life had to offer in order to follow the Gospel.

Bother Pachomius experienced support from the community, yet was keenly aware of his inability to respond to particular aspects of monastic discipline. It was a cause of consternation and compunction.

His key response, humbling as it might be, was honesty with an Abbot many years his junior: By asking for certain concessions while making real efforts to grow beyond these needs.

All of the elements of his desire came together less than a year ago when at the Feast of the Founders of Citeaux Brother Brother Pachomius was able to proclaim the totality of his single hearted fidelity by solemn profession, after so very many years as an Oblate. This was an event he constantly expressed gratitude about. It was an occasion when, in the words of the second reading, he could enter the freedom and splendor of the children of God. Now he has the full splendor of that life.

As the calendar year draws to a close, in the midst of celebrations filled with the humanness of the Holy Family and of the Birth of Christ, that solemnity which makes one very aware of family life. Brother responded to that final all embracing call and now knows the fullness of life.

—31 December 1978

The readings from Scripture (Job 19:23-27; Rom. 8:14-23; John 11:17-27) we have just heard, give us the strong encouragement of hope. The Gospel ended with Jesus' friend Mary, acknowledging Him as the Messiah, and so rests at peace regarding the life of Lazarus her brother. In the first reading the accused Job makes a strong profession of hope that the one who will defend his cause in the end is God, and with that defense Job will enter into the life which is God's very own.

The reading from Romans gives us a little of the other side of the picture. The hope which is God's Spirit given to us, is the call to life which keeps us from being victims of the futility to which creation was subjected. Another translation speaks of the created universe being made victim of frustration. For me this is an apt portrayal of Father Alfons' life — someone struggling not to succumb to the frustration of which he was victim. (But then too, he did succumb to making his Abbot an object of frustration!)

His experience of the futility to which the world is a victim started rather early in his life. As a young teenager he carried water to the Belgium troops during the First World War. He intimately experienced the injustice of wartime search parties and the exasperation of obtaining sufficient food. Partially to avoid such an experience again, his family emigrated to this country shortly after the war with all the insecurity that involves. In less than a year Father Alfons embraced monastic life at Gethsemani.

As a young monk he was zealous about his studies, manual labor and the life of the St. Benedict's Rule.

Father Alfons always had a great respect for Abbot Edmund Obrecht who had received him into monastic life and who had ordered the monastery in a very exacting way with minute rules to regulate every detail.

Perhaps because he never mastered the English language, or because he couldn't always handle the slight changes that occurred after the death of Dom Edmund, Father Alfons seemed to experience the futility to which all the universe has been made subject. He was taken seriously within the community. But the human heart, being endowed with the Spirit, which is one of hope and one that goes beyond frustration, develops a style of life that is more than the negative factors it experiences.

Father Alfons had a personality that was very much his own. While some of us as we entered were cheered in those early days by a rather rotund and robust older monk who looked at us with a broad smile and an impish glint in his eye, when we first arrived, Father Alfons always acknowledged our uniqueness. He tried to learn where we were from, what we did before entering. And accomplishing all that by using a sign language that seemed to be devised to frustrate personal communication.

Who among us did not enjoy a bit of the familiar, though worldly Christmas spirit, when Father Idesbald, as he was then known, would carry his laundry bag like Santa Claus' sack full of goodies, complexion ruddy and laugh jovial?

Though his position in the community was one of powerlessness, he tenaciously persevered and was exacting in his work, be it carpentry he loved, or the essential task of putting the exact quantity of salt on the cheese. His obligations to monastic life were always precise to the Rule.

Though he knew all the short cuts, the justice of the Chapter of Faults system, which seemed to respect persons and rank, always baffled him.

Although the Church of Vatican II appealed to Father Alfons, the preciseness of Dom Edmund Obrecht's time seemed more clear, more functional His sphere of responsibility within the community may have been severely limited, yet he always was interested in the life of the larger Church and the whole world. The election of Popes; the cardinals and their appointments, and the delight of having a Belgian Apostolic Delegate here in the States whom he met with great joy and animation, these were things his mind searched out.

The monks who were absent from the monastery for studies were always kept up on things of interest with letters from Father Alfons.

And the day it was announced that Father Louis had died in Bangkok, Father Alfons had just received the latest card in their ongoing communication.

Just a few evenings ago when visiting with Father Alfons,

his expressed concerns were of the Pope and his journey to Brazil. Then in a mixture of sign language and English he commented how it had always been the "old rule" that popes and the Trappists never travelled.

Now that the Pope is traveling, so soon the Trappists should travel. I, with the usual Abbot's incomprehension, spiritualized the meaning into his journey back to God. He, with the wisdom of life, gave a knowing chuckle.

As each of us endeavors to live our vocation "to be freed from the futility to which we are subject," we can't help but ask how others do it, and look to them for encouragement.

In Father Alfons, we see a tenacity and perseverance in situations far from congenial. We see a love of the Church and a concern for the poor of Christ. We see one who never spoke a word against another Brother. Then again, he wondered about preferential treatment by Superiors.

With Father Alfons, we also see one who took great joy in the little things of life, who, a few weeks ago, went in search of deer and merely to delight in the early summer of Kentucky.

As we commend our Brother to God we also must question how we assisted him to be freed from the futility of life? How did we respond to his concerns? In what way did we bring to him a sign of God's acceptance, a cause for hope? In many ways we have obviously failed; but God has provided him with family and friends who have always been a source of consolation and encouragement to him.

—24 July 1980

It is said that when friends asked the reason for his choosing monastic life, Brother Alexander expressed it in terms that today many would back away from. He wanted a life of penance. This, he obviously received with the physical burdens he carried from his first years here at Gethsemani.

First, there was the tuberculosis and the very serious operation in the early years of his monastic living which left a lasting effect.

Then there was the gradual debilitating effects from the Parkinson's disease that has been evident for twenty years or more.

Although these are things we would easily understand as penance, Brother's awareness was more profound. He knew his life's vocation of penance was the courage to fear God. The willingness to acknowledge the absolute, incomprehensible, holy God as the other to whom one relates in adoration.

Because of this, Brother recognized his complete dependence on this God of mercy and love. Even recent months speak of the life of penance. The Gospel we just read spoke of such as "blessed" because they are poor in spirit, because they mourn in the sense of being offended that God's name is not respected by all, they are the meek, those who are not aggressive for themselves.

Brother accepted his growing dependence on others despite his very strong natural tendencies to be independent. Being poor in spirit, meek and aware of God's glory, he knew he must receive. And so the receiving from his brothers for him was the sign of God's mercy coming. He was one of those rare persons who could receive love. This does not mean he couldn't on occasion let you know with a laconic phrase that you were being a bother.

Another element in Brother's life that brought him into the true life of penance was helping to bear the burden of sin that is evident in the general unhappiness and distress of the world. He was brought face to face with this during the many years as Porter and Gatekeeper at Gethsemani.

The porter's work brought him into contact with those in need in our neighborhood. It was Brother Alexander who distributed the weekly boxes of food. In this way he very visibly was aware of the distress of the world and this entered into not only his prayer, but also into his giving a good word and the assistance of the monastery, and always in the name of the community, not as a source of personal authority.

In addition to the fear of God, another of the qualifications St. Benedict lays down as essential for the Porter to be able to receive a message and respond to visitors. Brother Alexander was most capable in this area. Most met him as just a disembodied face in the small sliding window at the gate. On occasion my Mother, who for various reasons spent as little time as possible at the Ladies House, was at the Gatehouse waiting. Brother was trying to sweep up the area. My Mother got the message that she was in the way. She said she thought he would be happy to see her leave and so be out of his way. Brother said: "Yes, but the difficulty is that seven more, worse than the first, will arrive." Mother was never sure if that was a compliment or a put down.

A remembrance of Brother Alexander wouldn't be complete if we didn't mention his more than 35 years of service as the Harry Truman appointed Postmaster for Trappist KY. A more dedicated and faithful employee of the U.S. Postal Service would be difficult to find — nor a more ardent critic of U.P.S.

All these years as the Porter with its confused contact with many different characters certainly had its pressures. To be constantly vulnerable to the demands and questions of strangers is an expression of poverty that can only be built on a sure faith and living charity.

His life at the gate did not lead him away from the community. He never used the opportunities that were undoubtedly available to him to escape the discipline of living the Gospel that St. Benedict taught. He was always a monk. He delighted in lectio, and was ever faithful to his life of prayer and solitude in the cloister.

We all could not help but be strengthened by his continued faithfulness to the whole of his monastic life as his physical abilities became even more atrophied.

Brother Alexander will be missed, but even more the gentle man who knew how to take a message and give a response. He would smile with a child-like simplicity when he realized how far he had strayed from his own wishes and expectations. He was someone who had learned how to receive love because he was signed by the cross.

—5 March 1982

A few days before Christmas Brother Cyril made the long trip from the infirmary to the Abbot's office, pushing the wheel chair with various sundry pieces of cardboard and boxes, along with a copy of the *New Covenant* and the *Florida Catholic*. He said: "I just came over to do a bit of Christmas shopping." After getting together various papers and, turning the hearing aid just right, he continued: "Since it is probably going to be my last Christmas, I thought I should send a few extra gifts."

Brother Cyril had it all arranged. By sending smaller gifts he felt he could send more without too much extra cost. This completed, he went on to talk about Our Lady of Garabandal and other apparitions of Our Lady, and thought I just was not saying sufficient about what the Mother of the Lord was asking — prayer and penance. He added, "I should say more because some of the brothers don't get much chance to read about these here apparitions."

It seemed to me after my generosity with the extra Christmas gifts he could go a little easier on his criticism. But not Brother Cyril. There was a hierarchy of values. I just was not saying enough about prayer and penance.

To strengthen his point there were some quotes from Barclay's commentaries on the Gospel. Despite the fact that the quotes only made my position worse, it was good to hear that he was using the Commentaries that others have been waiting their turn for so long!

To take some of the focus off my failings I turned the conversation to his health. There were the problems with his feet. Despite his long experience as shoe maker and his making over ever pair of shoes he had bought from a magazine, he just couldn't get them right. Then there were the usual stomach complaints - nothing a little rhubarb and soda wouldn't fix! He then brought the conversation back to the Scriptures, the Book of Revelation, and offered a few insights. With that it was time to head back, but not before asking if it was all right to pray his Office of Our Fathers in his room since it was too difficult in the cold weather to get over to pray with the brothers.

This was Brother Cyril as most of us knew him, a person who embodied much that the Liturgy of the Word spoke to us about. Like Job he longed to see God and knew that he would.

Brother Cyril experienced himself caught in the growth pangs of the coming creation. But the suffering was not to be compared with the glory that was to come. Brother Cyril forgot his pains and longed to be involved in bettering creation by the many rosaries he prayed kneeling on his bed, by the sunflowers he planted, by the garden he was always planning to expand. He had a real awareness and concern about the life of the Church and that more and more people hear the Word of God and be acquainted with the Scriptures he so reverently read, always kneeling to read the first passages, always wanting to know what others thought about the meaning of various passages.

Yet still there was the experience of the pain, and he wasn't one to cover over his pain or discomfort. But in a simple direct statement, he would acknowledge the fact. A rather private person who was independent in his thoughts and needs. Always respectful of others, concerned with projects around the house, even willing to serve on committees, if the brothers would just talk so they could be heard!

—20 January 1982

All of us would knew Father Edward's little motto which he kept ever on his lips and even before his eyes — "GOD IS LOOKING ON."

Not God so much as judge, but God who was personally interested — the God of grace, the God of shared life, the God giver of all good gifts, the God spoken of in the Rule of Saint Benedict from whom we have strayed by disobedience and to whom we return by the labor of obedience, the God revealed in Jesus who emptied himself to be exalted to his Father's right hand, to send the Spirit into our hearts.

The beatitude we just heard — "Blessed are the meek for they shall possess the land" — summarizes Father Edward for me.

Certainly 97 years in this world indicates some type of "possessing the land!" But it is not so much the possession that is of interest to us, but rather the meekness, which is not a virtue we reflect on that often.

Meekness is a combination of humility and justice. It is not popular in our culture because it is the very opposite of the aggressiveness that is the mark of success.

In our midst these many years we have had one who showed us Jesus as meek and humble, who was like Moses in our midst because he was faithful in all things. The faithfulness, the perseverance, is the most obvious thing about Father Edward. To have entered the religious life at 13 and to be still doing it at 97 — or rather almost 98 — is no small thing.

Seventy of these years were spent here at Gethsemani. But it was not just perseverance, it is the quality of perseverance that is the important example for us. His perseverance wasn't just "hanging on;" it wasn't just a being here because he had no place to go, or it was too late to try something else — it was a creative perseverance that knows itself as responsible.

Father Edward was always interested in life; he was always seeking answers. He noticed things and remembered. Educator that he was, he always drew a lesson from every event, from every encounter. It was a perseverance that took responsibility for its life.

As with most of us, my first meeting with Father Edward was through the confessional screen; his words of a newly-arrived postulant were "to have a hobby" — even such a word as "hobby" in Gethsemani of 1958 sounded like blasphemy. But no, it was the true wisdom of the mature monk. It is saying: Be interesting in your surroundings, notice nature, love history, be responsible for your life. It is all God's, and if we don't put forth the effort to relate and love our world, the powers of evil will enter our minds and hearts. Just a few months ago he was telling me how important it was to control one's environment. For him it was to have pictures of nature and holy pictures around his desk, it was to have history books to read. Otherwise it was simple; the devil would get in. He always admonished his penitents to remember jokes in time of trial — nothing — nothing lightens the spirit more quickly. And just a few weeks ago he could say with an almost mischievous grin on his lips, that even at his age he could not let his thoughts run free. It is in this area where we he could say that Father Edward really encouraged certain culture within the Community — certainly not the highest form of culture, but you might call it the first stages of something more than a frontier settlement. How often he would use a quote from Shakespeare to underline a lesson, or a well-known verse from a famous poet. The highest compliment he could pay a person was to call him a gentleman. His interest in history was a great source of healthy distractions and lessons to be learned. There was France, the eldest daughter of the Church, and certainly no son gave a mother as much grief. Even France fell under the judgement reserved for the French, which was easy to give for a man whose name began with K— and ended with T— KNECHT, This gentleness and self-control that are the mark of the meek person, are also the sign of one who has received the gift of the Spirit, and are the traits we saw in Father Edward and in his constant example and counsel, of good-natured fidelity.

Meekness is not a kind of abnegation of all judgement, or denial of facts. When asked about life under the rather harsh regime of Dom Edmund Obrecht, Father Edward would never complain in vehemently, nor gloss over arbitrary actions.

Life under Dom Edmund was neither terrible or good. In Father Edward's judgement it was meritorious.

In other words, it was the individual monk who had to make it into something. It was using the dictum of St John of the Cross, who must put love into any situation. The times are to be redeemed by us. We are Christ's instruments. Passivity is not a trait of the meek.

Father Edward's monastic service to the Community has always been that of a person who is dependable and quietly fulfills his tasks without obvious accomplishments or the signs of authority.

He was the community's secretary and kept the records for years and years. It was Father Edward who corresponded with candidates in regard to documents. It was Father Edward who always offered a word of encouragement to the newly arrived postulant. He also conducted singing classes since 1918, and was Cantor between 1929 and 1950, a task in the days of showing "tablets" during the Office in order to correct the singing, a task which demanded a certain agility since the corrections were not always received in quiet humility.

In his correcting, there was nothing of arrogance in Father Edward, or impatience or anger. In recent years, he often commented on how much better the Community was without the Chapter of Faults, although he thought silence was the essence of the contemplative life and needed much improvement. But still, he saw charity now, and acknowledged the many acts of kind generosity towards himself—as real charity and something that a Chapter of Faults never created. In fact, all the changes of these later years were things he greeted with confidence and joy, frequently saying: "It should have been done many years ago." He clung to none of the things of the past as we often do; he was free in the sense that a truly poor man can be free.

His great devotedness to the Community showed in his faithfulness to the Office. He came to pray with the brethren until the physical impossibility was well beyond even a younger person's strength. His communal spirit was seen also in his interest in the novices of the Community, and in his trips to the work area even in his wheelchair to see if the first law of Heaven was being observed. All of us have heard that

"Order is Heaven's fundamental law, and cleanliness is next to Godliness" and for Father Edward these were the ways one showed his love for the brethren. This concern for the place, and love for his brothers, put him very much in the tradition of early Citeaux, and are the mark of a person thoroughly one with himself and with his vocation.

As well as we all knew Father Edward, there was something of a mystery about him, as there is about any person. What was behind all the evident good will, fidelity, and gentle service? Perhaps it is as simple as his spirit living so many years with full use of his faculties and his strong health. He freely acknowledged he did not know how he did it, he just received each day as God's gift with joy, with gratitude, and with creative fidelity.

—3 February 1983

"In all these things we are more than conquerors through him who loved us. " (Romans 8)

The liturgical day or season that a person completes his life is often something of a commentary on that life, and on what manner of response to the Spirit created in them by the Spirit. As it was proper for a Brother Jerome or a Brother Ferdinand to die during the Sacred Triduum, and for Brother Pachomius to be placed in the earth on Holy Family Sunday, for Father Louis to die the same date as his first arrival at the monastery during the Advent season with all its impatient longing and desire which were so much a part of Father Louis; so, too, for Brother Matthew, Christmas morning, when children are filled with excitement.

There really was something very boyish about Matt. The mere fact that we knew him by a name that wasn't his[1] (remember how as boys when we would play games making ourselves strange by a change of name or by taking up an attitude towards our surroundings that really wasn't ours, by claiming to have friends far beyond our social level), indicates that there was something very boyish in the fact that we knew Matthew Scott. He was really Rupert McGunigle.

He would look down upon us from behind powerful lenses due to his cataract operation, which in turn gave him a different optic of the world. He would often mention names that peopled movies and a world far beyond our experience. One was often tempted to think that Brother Matthew was playing a boyish game with us.

There were those frequent allusions to famous people whom he knew on a first name basis; yet when any one of us, or any group of us, tries to get them into a coherent story, it is very difficult.

The only solid fact that Dom James offered about Brother Matthew's life was given in something of an apologetic tone, and with a note of condescension in his voice. He'd say, "He attended that other school— Yale!"

Yet, these famous people who were his friends really were his friends. There were letters from these people— Ira Gershwin, Cary Grant, Bob Hope and Beatrice Lillie who mentions him in her autobiography as a very close friend, and many others. There was also the Duke of Windsor ("Eddie"), and those "disgusting nieces"— Elizabeth and Margaret, the former now being the Queen of England.

And it is true, if we would have read all the small print after the movies we would have seen the name "Rupert McGunigle". All these people, many of whom have kept some small contact with Brother Matthew were friends, but he left their world in 1949-1950.

A power of grace was at work within him. Brother Matthew entered the Church in 1949. None of us ever heard the story of the conversion, but perhaps it was the effect of his war experience as a First Lieutenant in the Air Force. He was there during the fire-bombing of Tokyo. He took the photographs of the first atomic bomb blast. Perhaps it was the grace from a life seriously lived, always searching for the Truth, or perhaps it was one of those dramatic turn-abouts. None of us knows for sure, because Brother Matthew was always a very private person.

He came to Gethsemani in 1950 with the desire to become a priest. But an earlier, short-lived marriage made the priesthood impossible. Brother Matthew always had a great attraction to the liturgical life— it was foundational in his early years at Gethsemani, and again when he returned to the regular life after living in the Guesthouse for a short period. It was the Liturgy that was at the heart of his desire to return, the communal aspect of it, the climate it created. His return to the regular life from the Guesthouse was also a conversion experience. The letter he wrote to Father Flavian was a deeply personal document, at least by allusion, and shows a real deep self-knowledge, and also an experience of the need for prayer and the power that the Lord Jesus can work in the heart of a person who longs for the Truth. He stated this in terms of the pride and arrogance that were things that kept him separated from the love of God.

Soon after returning to the regular life failing eyesight and a loss of hearing made active liturgical participation impossible.

Also, the Liturgy was no longer in the classical language that he loved so much, and certainly Liturgy in anything but Latin in Matt's terminology was nothing but "kid's stuff ! " As his physical condition and the changing climate of the Community developed, Matthew lived more and more a private life. Yet he was always in contact, praying the Hours when the Community prayed, being very conscientious about his work with the Mass stipends, or taking pictures of communal events, or providing photographs for those who asked, or keeping his well-arranged photo archive in excellent condition. He was always a person who used his time well in private study of the Scriptures, re-reading the classics of English literature. He always had an inquisitive mind, was always learning, always interested in persons and events.

All this bore fruit in great expressions of gratitude that were his constant conversation these last several days. That is the sign of the poor man, from the opening phrase of our Gospel text this afternoon. It is the poor in spirit to whom the Kingdom of God is given. The poor person is the person who can express genuine gratitude, and the one who expresses genuine gratitude is the one who knows his poverty and that all is from "the victory of Him Who loved us." Father Louis always said that a true contemplative was the one whose life was nothing but an expression of gratitude. And the child that we love is the one who can say a genuine thanks with the freedom of a real child.

That is all that Matt could say these last days at the hospital. When any of us visited him, he was always expressing his gratitude for all that had been done for him and for the fact that someone would think of stopping to see him at the hospital. Christmas Eve afternoon during a short visit with him, after his return from the hospital, he was full of gratitude for "these wonderful guys; it was so good to be back in their midst." He looked forward to Midnight Mass and at the exchange of peace, he offered his peace to as many as possible, and was delighted with all the brothers who came to him; he was grateful for his early morning coffee, and "the breakfast of a king" as he said it was, and it was probably with a wonder and a loud laugh that he opened his eyes to the Christmas Tree which is lighted in Eternity and will never be extinguished.

Brother Matthew was really our little Brother— certainly much more mature and intelligent than most of us, but a Brother who always knew his needs, was always faithful to his conversion, always using his gifts of intellect ... He always suffered from a very strong temper, which he always labored to direct and control. Yet he did a masterful job in making this force in his life always a force for good.

—25 December 1983

[1] Brother Matt was only known as Matt Scott by members of the community.

FATHER JOHN GRAF

To say something appropriate for Father John, it should be done in sign language or at least with many grand gestures pointing with the index finger saying "Mitre bearer," "Crozier bearer," "Kiss the ring first, " Having been Master of Ceremonies for so many years, most of us experienced this rather formidable monk looking out from under bushy eyebrows with a resolute composure that would cause a lapse in rubrical memory even in the most astute liturgist.

Resolute is possibly the proper word to describe Father John's composure, since he was a rather tense person with a severe speech defect that caused a real breakdown in communication when he was asked something without being prepared, or when forced to move from a prepared script. Undoubtedly, it was this burden that was in part the cause of his leaving his first vocation as a Marianist Brother. He had entered the brothers at age 13, and left 7 years later, while teaching 6th grade boys. He worked as an accountant for a couple of years before entering the Abbey of Gethsemani. It was during the years as a Marianist that Father John and our late Father Edward first knew one another. It was a relationship that continued at least to the extent of a weekly confession to Father Edward, and anyone else within earshot, until Father Edward's death. Very deaf Father John speaking to hard-of-hearing Father Edward made for an entertainment comparable to the best TV can offer.

Resolute Father John was in all his life, more in the sense of faithful than just firm determination. These last many years— maybe as many as 20— of residency in the infirmary because of high blood pressure, were not simple years for a monk like Father John. To be waited on, to be served, was not something he accepted with ease, although he did receive it with gratitude. The regular community life was a real part of Father John's spiritual way, so to be separated from it was an experience of exile. The separation didn't cause Father to lose interest in the brethren. He avidly read the bulletin board (in the dark in order to save electricity) and always asked about monks he no longer noticed during his daily peregrinations, clicking his cane, and turning off lights as he steadily plodded along. Neither did his enforced hermit's life cause him to forget his brothers, nor did the almost absolute deafness cause Father John to become a suspicious, if not paranoid, person, which so often happens with persons who lose their hearing late in life. Perhaps this freedom in the midst of even his loss of hearing was because of the depths of his own self-forgetfulness. He never expressed any concern for himself beyond the fear of being a burden to someone else. Thus, there was no chance for a paranoid response to a community he could not hear.

Perhaps this element of freedom in his life, this lack of self-centered concern, was the expression of the monk who so obviously lived the principles the Liturgy of the Word offered us this morning— the name of the Father, the source of all glory, which Jesus revealed to his disciples, so that they, so that we, could know the same love— was Father John's one desire. The scrupulousness that was a part of the burden in his resolute living was an accepted way for him to show the single-hearted response of his love. His exactness in celebrating Mass lengthened it to such an extent as to cause a crisis in a Mass server's life were he to have Father John two weeks in a row. This however was but an expression of his resolute desire to return a total love for a total gift of life.

This same love that the reading from Romans tells us is the Spirit who teaches us to pray: "Abba, Father" was the spirit of prayer Father John constantly desired.

When did one ever find him reading anything other than a Bible, spiritual books, or notes gleaned from spiritual readings and developed into pious meditations, a few of them being published in Monastic Exchange?

Even his confessor couldn't turn him from his singly directed reading. Father Edward told of giving Father John a beautiful calendar with pictures of Ireland. The calendar was returned with a note that he (Father John) only looked at holy pictures— his name being Graf, Ireland didn't qualify as holy.

But all the pictures that Father John saw weren't that holy.

I must admit to having a bit of resentment towards Father John. A few years ago I happened to hear from an old college girlfriend, and she inquired whether I ever got the picture she sent me when I was a novice, and I had to answer not only did I not receive the picture, but I didn't even get the letter. I kind of resented Father John for this — just think, my whole life might have been different if John had not censored the mail so well!

That, too, is probably part of the reason why only spiritual reading interested him. He must have been awfully bored hearing of Aunt Mary's arthritis, Uncle Charlie's refusal to have anything to do with A.A., and St. Anne's failure to find a man for cousin Jeanne.

Father John did long that all things be made new as the reading from Revelations spoke of, but it wasn't from a despising of the world. A man of such obvious detachment interestingly made a real effort in the various room changes he made through the years in the infirmary, to always have a view of natural beauty and he always arranged his furnishings to take advantage of the scene.

When the boundaries of our enclosure were expanded to include much more territory, on occasion I would meet Father John in full habit on the Linton Farm.[2]

One clear, cold, crisp, snowy Sunday in January I remember him watching former Brother Celsus from a bluff overlooking the bottoms, as Brother traced a gigantic circle in the unadulterated snow with the spokes leading into the center, the type of track we used to play fox and goose as boys.

If sign language would have been more ample, perhaps I could have convinced Father John to enter the game, but then that would have been bad for his heart.

What more do these few, almost insignificant events, tell us about his life other than its humility? Certainly Father John could not appreciate all this attention being given to him.

A monk who was so resolute and self-forgetting — jubilee days were not even to be mentioned, visitors were never invited back, and correspondents were told not to write, and to expect no further responses. He would appreciate the brothers who gathered to celebrate the Conventual Mass which he attended when it was at a proper time. He would be disappointed at the lack of rubrical exactness — he gave up pointing out my blunders a few years ago — but he could accept that. He would very much expect our prayers for him, claim his need for them. Father John was a man who was inwardly burdened. He never hesitated to acknowledge to his abbot,

84

several years his junior, his trials and difficulties. This indeed was practicing the humility that the Rule of Benedict calls the monk to in order to be faithful to Christ.

Father John, or Brother John, or simply John, as he signed his communications these last few years, should give us hope. He followed the monastic way of Gospel living with resoluteness that is beyond the strength of most of us; yet he always remained fully human, aware of life, accepting of the foibles of others, and constant in his single-hearted dedication. The Eucharist was the center of his life, not just in its liturgical celebration, but by letting the death of Jesus be realized in him by absolutely leaving all, especially his own will and desires, in order to be signed with the love of Jesus.

—25 April 1985

2A monastic property a half mile from the monastery, once occupied by the Linton family.

BROTHER CASPAR DEVER

Brother Caspar came to the community as a late vocation— at 46— saying the car he drove in the mid-fifties, was a symbol of his life. It was a Studebaker and its design made the back and the front appear very similar, so there were all these jokes about not knowing which way the car was going. Caspar confessed his own life had that quality.

But the statement was something of an Irish hyperbole, since Brother's life was directed very strongly in caring for an aging parent, being very active in parish life, especially in the choir at St. Clare's Church, where I suspect he learned to be about one beat ahead of everyone on entering a musical phrase.

In his generosity to various communities of nuns and other community services, in his being a friend of all, an easy touch for a little something to hold one over till payday - in all this Brother Caspar was always on the way, but was so much a part of the way, that he didn't recognize his direction or position.

The same simple Christian way marked his life among us— getting Brother Dominic in the wheelchair and showing him other parts of the monastery, mixing cement when he wasn't cooking soup, (Brother Caspar always being the first to notice the analogies between jobs). Carrying the biggest, heaviest haybales on the hottest day to the highest loading wagon; helping out wherever and whenever it was asked; putting together boxes for the poor of the neighborhood and finding in this a real identity with God's special people. He took care of the calves to encourage Brother Ferdinand — except that sometimes Brother Ferdinand worried because "Everything that comes into that Brother's head comes out his mouth. " Then Brother Ferdinand would add: "...and a lot of times it shouldn't!"

But Brother Caspar was there to care, and also to find an audience for a few of his antics which were generally stories where he would laugh at himself and express his gratitude for all the opportunities God had given him and the many times he was saved from himself.

Brother Caspar's questions were always in search of the truth — always he wanted to learn, to take an active part in classes, to read dense philosophical tomes.

Which one of us hasn't laughed to see his wheelchair filled with the Summa, Biblical commentaries, philosophical books, and — the touch of true Caspar — a few National Geographics shoved in-between to express his most basic concern — the well-being of other people? He wanted to understand, he desired to know and he took pleasure in being lost in a book.

His personal copy of the Bible is glossed in the New Testament, and the flyleaves are filled with scrolls, quotations from other books.

The life that Brother Caspar so desired was the radical commitment to the Gospel. He left all for the sake of the Lord. Truly, he did not want to live his own life, but he wanted Christ to live in him.

Brother Caspar had a war story that convinced him of the value of obedience. Master Machinist Mate 1st class of the U.S. Navy Robert Dever[3], was successfully landing troops on D-Day. When darkness caused him to return with a group, they demanding to get off at the first transport available, Brother Caspar refused saying that orders were to return to the assigned ship. Arriving at their proper ship, the Infantry told the little sailor what they were going to do to him.

Brother Caspar was saved from their wrath by the sound of the explosion that sunk the ship that everyone had to board! Obedience saved his life in a very literal sense. That is what Brother always sought, even in the midst of suffering debilities from Parkinson's disease. He always wanted to serve, always wanted to obey, was always alert, always grateful.

But the obedience part wasn't always simple for one with the strong will Brother Caspar had. He told one brother that he decided to leave this place at least 20 times a day in order to persevere.

What is the old saying some of us have heard about tempered steel? —the strongest metal is tempered metal, but when it loses its temper it is useless.

Caspar was tempered steel, and he lost it on occasion only to regain its strength by his genuine remorse and his ability to laugh at himself. The power of his temper was the strength of all his emotions; the gratitude he would often express for all that he had received; the frustration and concern about being a burden; at being reminded of what he was to do; the exasperation that this caused; the fears and anxieties of a very independent person now totally dependent.

Brother Caspar had always been thorough and didn't like to be pushed. Like that other bit of homespun philosophy, "As you live, so shall you die." So Caspar wasn't going to be pushed even in death.

Brother had come to monastic life "to be crucified with Christ for the destruction of the sinful self" as the reading from Romans stated it. And so he celebrated Holy Week in his very personal way as he quietly and calmly went about the process of going to the Lord at his own pace. Undoubtedly he was sorting out the many questions he wanted answered before any final commitment on his part.

And it was only on the evening of the Resurrection after the Lord had appeared to the disciples hidden in fear, only after he proclaimed His peace that Caspar could say: "Let's go." And I suspect when he opened his eyes in those last few moments of his life, it was as he was putting his hands in the side and his fingers in the place of the nails.

—9 April 1985

[3]Brother Casper's name in civilian life.

The death of a Christian is always uniquely individual; yet it is an event of the Community.

This, in a very particular way, is true for Father Augustine who was always a unique individual; yet his dying had a quality of Community seldom experienced.

It seemed that for a person who always labored to bring to perfection any talent he might have (even going so far as learning Gaelic in his mid-eighties) that our gracious God in these weeks brought to light a dimension of Father Augustine that had to be perfected for him to be truly a whole person. As his condition weakened a few weeks ago, each of us was called to be with him and serve this very private person in a manner most thought impossible. Yet our ministrations were easily accepted and I believe often recognized so that our bond of fraternity was beyond our own capabilities.

A simple recital of all Father Augustine's experiences and accomplishments would take us long past sunset. It also would really create a wrong picture of this man who in reality was seeking but one thing: The love of God which is the life of Jesus in each one of us.

The quote from St. Paul to the Corinthians that begins the autobiography he began to write several months ago indicates his approach — "Whether you eat or drink, or whatsoever you do, do all for the Glory of God."

And so Father Augustine lived; all was for the Glory of God and all would enhance God's Glory.

Father was from the Old European gentry which colored his perceptions of life. He was also part of the New World aristocracy, being an engineer and lawyer in Argentina.

An English gentleman in a Trappist monastery in backwoods Kentucky is material for a novel, but it is not necessarily an uncomplicated life to live — the ways of these Americans can be a bit uncouth!

As one hears of the exotic places, the historically significant times, the engrossing professional careers that made up Father Augustine's life, it would seem that his life was the fullest of lives, even beyond our imaginings.

Yet, it was personally a very sad life, filled with the radical failures that demand one to seek that deeper life that is the only true life. A family business caught in the complications of European nationalism, an education in an alien environment, the confusion of World War I England, the loss of a leg, and a marriage that ended in heart break.

Yet Father Augustine was a person who constantly searched further. He entered the Roman Catholic Church at the end of World War I. In the late 1940s he began his studies for ordination in Argentina, and entered Gethsemani in the mid fifties.

Always searching, always trying to discover his potential, Father was never idle. He searched Eastern Religions and tried their detailed practices, always in the context of his Christian belief, always pushing to stretch his boundaries.

It was a couple of summers ago on the occasion of speaking with the Tibetan Buddhist monks who visited here that Father's questions began coming together. The Tibetans assured him in their tradition, too, the individual person continues a distinctive life even in the life of Buddha— as Jesus said in our Gospel: "Let the love with which you loved me be in them so that I may be in them. "

With that Father Augustine's life had a new elan . Perceptively more peace came into his everyday living. He began giving away various possessions which he now knew to be unnecessary. He had done so much for so many of us as counselor and confessor and spiritual guide; yet after this, he became even more effective.

During his whole monastic life Augustine was the most able guide and interpreter of life's ups and downs, seeing the burdens as a way to make up in our personal lives the sufferings that would complete the redemptive work of Christ in us.

He was always a patient listener. He would be there Saturday after Saturday hearing confessions in the back of the Church, and was always willing to give a retreatant extra time. He was always willing to help a person interpret his life history. And so he developed many deep personal friendships.

—9 September 1985

90

BROTHER MAURUS GOMEZ

Yesterday as we celebrated the Liturgy of the Dedication of the Church, with its use of the Jacob story regarding the ladder set up between heaven and earth, and the angels descending and ascending, another story of the patriarch Jacob came to mind as I looked at Brother Maurus lying in the bier with the paschal candle at one end and the cross at the other.

Remember Jacob alone at the ford of the river, and a man wrestled with him until daybreak? As Chapter 32 of the Book of Genesis describes it: "When the man saw that he could not throw Jacob, he struck him in the hollow of the thigh so that Jacob's hip was dislocated as they wrestled. The man said, 'Let me go, for day is breaking'.

"But Jacob replied, 'I will not let you go unless you bless me'. He said to Jacob, 'what is your name'". And he answered, 'Jacob'.

"Then the man said, 'your name shall no longer be Jacob, but Israel, because you strove with God, and with man and prevailed . '

"Jacob said, 'Tell me your name. ' He replied, 'why do you ask my name?"... and did not give him his name, but his blessing.

"Jacob called the place 'Penuel' 'because,' he said, 'I have seen God face to face, and my life is spared.' The sun rose as Jacob passed through Penuel, limping because of his hip.'"

And so the story ends, but it has remained throughout the history of civilization, as have accounts of God's special messengers, limping through history because of their encounter with God, but always carrying a special message, which is for the hope and salvation of all.

Brother Maurus is one who wrestled with God and was marked with one of those very particular vocations to share in the mystery of suffering. Like the patriarch Jacob, he was debilitated by his encounter, and like all those who have come down to us in history, he carried a very special message for us.

Very soon after Brother Maurus' arrival at Gethsemani in the 1930s, a most basic renunciation was demanded of him.

Dom Edmond Obrecht could read many languages, but could not read Spanish, and because he wasn't allowed any letters directed to him that were uncensored, he received none at all.

With that obedience to the Rule, Brother lost the joy of communicating in his own language.

A few weeks before Brother Maurus's ordination to the priesthood, he suffered an attack of epilepsy which was an impediment for him to continue to orders. Thus, he was called to share the priesthood in a different way. He was irrevocably called into the mystery of suffering, and so signed with the cross of Jesus. And given a priestly mission to call each of us into the mystery of the cross.

Though the sacramental service of ordained minister was not to be his, Deacon Maurus' whole life was to be identified with the ministry of the Lord Jesus, and to be a living proclamation of the Gospel.

For almost fifty years he lived the mystery of powerlessness. During many of these years, Brother lived the regular monastic life, with the ups and downs of poor health. For a long time, he was hospitalized, then he was confined to a wheelchair with the frustrating burden of being completely dependent for the most elemental human needs.

As our reading from the letter to the Romans (Roman 8 14-23) describes the universe living in hope, longing to be freed to enter upon the liberty and splendor of the children of God, so Brother Maurus lived in hope.

We all long for the same fulfillment, but for Brother Maurus it was a case of always living in that one particular condition of hoping for the fulfillment of the Lord.

His being signed with the mystery of the cross included all the experiences that are part of any monastic consecration to God. He even wondered about his life of celibacy, and on occasion would question rather insistently if he should not be married.

The loneliness and frustration, and the poverty of dependence, the confusion and incomprehension, were all a part of Brother Maurus' vocation. Still, he accepted his situation and lived in it.

He had the freedom to appreciate the brothers who would play checkers with him, and the freedom to demand that he win; he enjoyed the parcels and letters from his family, and still more their thoughtful visits. And he had that greatest of monastic virtues- he loved ice cream and everything sweet.

Brother Maurus has been for us a living of the Gospel message we heard read—the grain of wheat must die to bear a harvest; to serve the Lord Jesus one must be in the same place as Jesus, doing the will of the Father; accepting the call in absolute dependence on God, a dependence that is ministered by his brothers. Brother Maurus had the unique vocation to proclaim the message of Jesus' suffering in our midst. He called us to recognize our own needs, our own powerlessness. It is not a simple mission to call others to share in the cross of Christ, yet it is the greatest of vocations, since there is no other way.

—16 November 1987

If there was an image needed to describe Brother Wilfrid, I would think of him as the court jester. You know the person at the King's court who could say and do the most outlandish things and get away with them.

Yet what was uttered and done was often a most pointed criticism of the King and his policies, a devastating comment about something held in reverence, a word that uncovered the barren truth of life.

For many of us Brother Wilfrid was that character, that jester, that clown. He was eager to share a family visit, or make remarks to visitors that always had a shock effect and often a barb that tore both ways.

One could not help but feel that this ready humor and quick wit and that desire for an audience, were cover-ups for someone who knew the roots of frustration threatening to overpower a sensitive and fragile person who suffered deeply.

The gray mastic tape and magic markers that were the tell-tale signs that Brother Wilfrid had been there. The contact paper and extremely sentimental pictures of Jesus, all spoke of an effort to control and support a nature that knew the sufferings that awaited before God's spirit would be free to pray in the depth of his heart, Abba, Father.

Brother Wilfrid was the most unlikely candidate for a monastery known for its strict observance in the 1950s, having been a brother in a nursing community for over thirty years.

His letter of request for entering only asked to have "a life of strict penance for my own life and also to help others, thereby."

Perhaps he got more than he could handle, the silence, the austere piety, the formality were irksome for one who always had a remark, and who loved votive lights and flowers—real or paper—and thrived on practical jokes. Much of this joy of life found some outlet in the context of serving in the infirmary and lightening the life of many a staid brother, and adding a bit of personal warmth in a rather bleak context as a sign of the Kingdom of God about to break through.

Brother Wilfrid came before the test of the true monk, a call that every serious Christian must respond to, the call to go beyond all that is cherished in the best and dearest way.

Brother was called to give up the obvious evangelical work of directly serving the sick, not only when transferring from his original religious community, but even the service of the sick he had within our community. He was called to do other simple tasks within the community.

It was not an easy surrender for Brother Wilfrid.

And it has taken years, and the support of various brothers who would patiently hear Willie out in the midst of deep frustration.

As we all know, and as we all must experience, it is only when we have received the ministrations mentioned in the Sermon on the Mount that we are truly followers of Christ—only when our poverty is being ministered to, not just when we are giving to others; only when we are being consoled, not just giving consolation, and so on, only then are we truly disciples of the Lord Jesus.

So, Brother Wilfrid who had ministered to so many, had to receive, had to be supported and encouraged, had to freely receive the love of Christ from his brothers.

These ministrations Brother learned to receive with a gentleness, with a cooperation and gratitude that were signs of this world being freed from the shackles of mortality and entering upon the liberty and splendor of the children of God.

We should say more about the brother who still received messages from patients he assisted fifty years ago; of the musical talent that caused some difficulties; of the respect for the regular life in the midst of his rather flamboyant style—he respected and was faithful to the structured life of prayer; his devotion to his baptismal patron St. Joseph, on whose Feast Wilfrid was brought gently and peacefully into the Kingdom. But rather than say more, let us simply do what Wilfrid would want us to do, to share in the banquet of this Kingdom, to share the very life of the Lord Jesus, and be grateful for Brother Wilfrid, and his jesting and his care for us, grateful for his receiving the mercy of God through us and for us.

—21 March 1988

Perhaps the question in the second reading from Paul to the Romans: "What can separate us from the live of Christ?" says a great deal about our Brother Odilo — about his hope and more particularly about his fear that he might be separated from the love of God.

To reflect a little on Brother Odilo's life and how it can call us further into Gospel living is a rather formidable task. There are reams of his long essays which, in order to read demand a certain distancing from one's sensitivity to correct grammar and to the usual format of an essay. Their subject matter ranges from scientific investigation into the life cycle of grackles, that bird that endears itself by its screech and droppings, to obtuse metaphysical reflections of life's most basic questions.

Then there are didies about various things. The written legacy is one thing, then there are the tapes!

One can scan a paper, but how does one scan a tape by Brother Odilo without missing something? There is Odilo, for instance, singing a voice-over with Pavarotti; there is Odilo doing a duet with Judy Garland in "Somewhere Over the Rainbow"; to be followed by some dense philosophical theology on the topic of that tension we live with which is fundamentally the experience of our call to the transcendent. "Our hearts are always looking for more." That is Odilo: The tension he lived with which was his call to know the transcendent love which is the very life of God.

Far be it from me to criticize the Lord, but one felt that the pieces that composed Andrew Michael Waldrom, Brother Odilo, just didn't fit together. The body and psyche were just not up to containing the Spirit with its unbounded yearning for the fullness of God's love. As a result there were tensions which, in the merciful love of the Lord, were Odilo's special way to the fullness of life. As the reading from Roman's said: In spite of all, victory is ours through him who loves us." Brother Odilo's life of searching began early, one might almost call it a maverick life since it never really accepted traditional boundaries. Odilo never quite meshed with the structure of school.

He was in the Army at the end of WWII, transportation division, and his vehicle was never quite in line; he worked on the sugar docks in Brooklyn and that is where he learned to run.

Apparently the stevedores didn't always appreciate his humor. During all this time he was searching for that other dimension. Always a faithful Irish Catholic in the days long before the ecumenical movement, he would nevertheless drive his model A Ford from church to church and take part in various church services, only to be penalized by the priest at his next confession. He did have some difficulty about wearing the skull cap at the synagogue.

He excused himself from the Church's strictures regarding the YMCA because he needed to strengthen his body for self defense at work on the docks. All this was in search of some way to respond to the burning which he literally experienced in the depths of his being.

He was a Benedictine novice, only to experience the desire for that something more which brought him to Gethsemani.

His life with us here has been a continued search, a continued questioning. With good cause we always categorized him as an innocent child. This he was in many ways, but more probably because he never was a child really and had become street-smart at an age when many still play in sandboxes.

He had a child's fascination with nature. He worried about whether the birds would get enough to eat on a snowy winter day; whether the dry summer would be difficult for the deer nearby. And worried about natural catastrophes, about individuals who suffered personal tragedies. He would speculate how they would cope. He worried about brothers who left monastic life and feared he would too.

Most of all, he worried that he was a burden to his brothers because of his physical and psychic handicaps. He worried because he wanted answers to questions that have no answers, and some of us were short with him on occasion when he persisted with his questions.

He loved people — in a distant way. For years he worked in the guest house and gave the retreatants tours of the monastery. But always he was seeking the answer to the questions. He would furtively make friends with guests, seeking liberation from confusion with the questions he carried within himself. How did others answer them? He soon discovered many did not even ask such questions!

In some sense the whole of life's project seemed to be falling apart on him these last several months. He knew the basic dynamic of growth. At bottom, death is the way to life.

So Brother Odilo asked, with a certain calm resoluteness, for the kind of psychological help he always literally ran from. He submitted himself totally and was beginning to experience some liberation in accepting reality when he received a premonition of a virus that would kill him from inside - a premonition that in God's mercy became true.

Now Brother Odilo's questions will be no more; now his concern for others, for the little creatures of nature will be at peace; now the burning fire he knew in his depths will be one with the eternal love of God.

— 18 August 1988

One evening a couple of weeks ago on my way from the office to my room, I noticed the light on in the tailor shop.

Thinking Father Matthew was giving ghostly counsel, I went on, only to wonder, doubt and come back to check. There was Brother Octavius at his sewing machine, possibly fabricating his shroud. He asked what he could do for me.

I asked why he was working then. It was 9:15 p.m. He said that was impossible.

"Look out the window, it is getting dark," I said.

He then told me he had just noticed that and thought maybe there was a miracle. He questioned me about whether I were certain it was night. He then accepted my assurance, and with a sprightly step, went off to bed after lecturing me on the importance of work.

Gethsemani lost someone very unique to its history with the death of Brother Octavius, who still thought in German, and loved to make his Cologne accent ever so obvious.

Something of the international flavor that was evident in the community even in the 1950s is disappearing.

Not just a linguistic culture is being lost, but persons who had a certain experience of life, knew the discipline of a craft, and possessed the ingenuity necessary to survive in a new culture.

Brother Octavius' way was to be totally present to wherever he was and whatever he was doing. This is not to lessen his interest in other places and other people, but he was present, very present to you when speaking with you; very present to this place in wanting to know its news and its possibilities; very present to other people and their histories.

When Octavius was in the tailor shop, he was there actively involved in keeping everything in good German order. When he was in the hospital he was truly there, learning the ins-and-outs of its practical arrangements, and the life stories of all the nurses in attendance. When he had a trip to the doctor, dressed with his blue tie and dark glasses, he felt it must be a true "journey," and he would see all there was to see within bounds—although these bounds were not scrupulously kept. And when there were visitors from abroad, no tourist firm could equal Brother Octavius' ability to organize in detail a total experience of a place and its history.

This virtue of being totally present was not without its dark side. Brother Octavius was intensely present, with a vigor and a strength that could go awry. Ask anyone who was on the other end of a cross-cut saw from him!

Then there was that frightful accident, when possibly from over-driving a team of horses, he fell under the wagon and had multiple injuries to his legs and pelvic area. This was at a time when the medical profession was not too adept at caring for such complexities.

Perhaps that accident was result of a vigor for living that was so much Brother Octavius' way.

Yet, with a strength of will and a love of life, he recuperated and continued to live a rather complete monastic observance, ever conscious and careful of the precarious state of his legs, which the doctors claimed he would lose, but which he brings with him to the grave.

This delicate state of health never hindered his living a life with fullness and interest. Our reading from Philippians (3:20-21) with its promise of a transfigured body was always a source of hope for Brother Octavius.

Brother began his tourist ways as a young man whose family supported his love of new peoples and places.

As the political climate became more complicated in the Germany of the 1930s, Octavius left for Holland. Then to England. Then ultimately to this country, where he became a Franciscan Brother in a group with a nursing apostolate.

From that community he came to Gethsemani. He returned to Europe and worked at our Order's Generalate throughout the 1950s. When his health weakened and he was to return to the States, his inclination was to go the monastery of Mariawald in Germany.

Brother Octavius returned to the United States and made tentative arrangements to return to Mariawald, but his health prevented it.

What brought this well-to-do young German to enter a nursing order, then to transfer to a cloistered, penitential order in a strange land in troubled times, we can only conjecture. The structure of his life of devotion can be found written in the well- formed script of an educated European, along with the recipes he had devised while cooking for the guests here at Gethsemani.

Brother Octavius prayed the Stations frequently each day, was faithful to all his offices, and visited the cemetery daily; he

On doctor appointment days he prayed the whole office before leaving the monastery. He was faithful and regular at the Eucharist, and with the same presence he brought to all of life, led the responses and was the first to communicate.

It is interesting to see the influence of Vatican II in Brother Octavius's private notebook: He studied all the various world religions and made notes of their statistics and outlines of their beliefs. He was proud of his relatives in Germany, and was sure that his priest-nephew would be Pope, which he is undoubtedly trying to arrange at this moment!

He so wanted all to experience life totally. And this life experience was not a formless wandering, but purposefully directed: Filled with order, filled with the beauty of children and Renaissance presentations of the Virgin and Child; filled with color travel brochures of exotic places; filled with work that could be completed; filled with the joy of new people with stories of new places; filled with lots of sugar and well prepared food — but never any fish!

—13 September 1988

While praying psalms with Brother Joseph at Brother Stephen's side this morning, the vacuum cleaner in the tribune drowned us out every few minutes. It seemed fitting.

Nothing delighted Brother Stephen more — perhaps even more than psalms — than a well cleaned floor or a corridor with even the tops of the door lintels bathed in furniture polish! Of the many mansions promised in the Gospel, certainly Brother Stephen's would have to be dust free. Or better still, someone else's mansion needing to be cleaned, would surely be the greatest joy for him.

It was difficult to be Brother Stephen's abbot. He was too good. Listened too well. Obeyed too exactly. Loved trials too ardently. There surely must be a level of monk between Brother Stephen's over-exactness, self-effacing generosity, punctuality, and say Brother —. We will not mention any names, since too many of us fall on that other side of the scale.

Reading the Instruments of Good Works in the Rule of Saint Benedict one can see Brother Stephen and the source of his inspiration. "First of all, love the Lord God with your whole heart, your whole soul and all your strength...; you must honor everyone, renounce yourself in order to follow Christ; discipline your body, do not pamper yourself, but love fasting...; help the troubled and console the sorrowing; refrain from too much eating or sleeping and from laziness; ...if you notice something good in yourself, give credit to God, not to yourself." And so on. Brother Stephen was an exacting disciple who heard the word with zeal and did it without reserve. In the midst of his own rigidity there was always a largeness of heart for the rest of us that ever called him to our service no matter how undeserving we were; ever made him forgetful of self, no matter how much he suffered, and ever identified him with the Cross of the Lord Jesus.

When we reflect on how others live the Gospel in an effort to deepen our own conviction, we cannot help but be in that conundrum of wondering what is grace and what is nature; where is the folly of the Cross, and where the obstinacy of will that is ego and not self- surrender. And Brother Stephen's life offers no easy clue to this difficult discernment.

Brother Stephen was the only child of older parents. His father died while Stephen was young. He was raised by his mother and her parents, being taught from earliest youth to help clean, respect one's elders, and never be idle. He was a postulant with the Passionists in Louisville, but did not become a novice for rather unclear reasons. He had to return to the Cincinnati area to assist his mother, and was not invited to return to the novitiate. Perhaps he had a Trappist leaning even in those times.

The austerity of Gethsemani, coupled with Brother Stephen's fragile health, made the possibility of becoming a Trappist very remote.

Instead, he became a Benedictine at St. Bernard's in Cullman, Alabama, where his generosity and selfless service toward visitors, students, and the community, were something of a legend.

Friends from those years of thoughtfulness and generosity are with us today, and they remember Brother Stephen as this thoughtful and generous monk.

During difficult times for the community at St. Bernard's, it was Brother Stephen who was a source of strength and inspiration with his unperturbed faith and service to all. Ultimately, he was given permission to enter the post-Vatican II Gethsemani, after over thirty years as a Benedictine. He has been with us for more than twenty years, supporting and encouraging and serving.

St. Paul tells us our sufferings are nothing compared to the splendor that we can expect from this gracious God. Brother Stephen, like many others among us, seemed to establish an equation of proportion between suffering and glory to be given. To receive freely, to receive graciously, to receive humbly is the greatest and perhaps only sign of the fullness of discipleship. This was difficult for Brother Stephen.

Though quick to give mitigation to others, nothing was ever given to himself by way of food, comfort, or respect. His greatest concerns, even during the last weeks, were the burdens he may be causing others. To receive freely was difficult for Brother Stephen.

I like to think that the words given to Brother while anointing him a few hours before his passage into eternity were understood and accepted as the call to the ultimate conversion. Brother Stephen was urged to relax, to let go, and to receive the Lord who was coming to be the fullness of his life.

I do believe Brother in his ultimate desire to be obedient received these words with an open heart. He always wanted the fullness of Christ's life. He was an example of the danger a teacher or spiritual guide must be aware of. The proclamation of the Gospel must always be given to the individual person.

The same size does not fit all.

We are all called to receive the fullness of Christ's life, but the how is a little different for each of us, and it is essential that we hear and be encouraged to listen to the word that is particular to our way of being disciples.

—27 April 1989

104

FATHER PHILIP RICHERT

The beatitudes of the Gospel today perhaps best summarizes Father Philip's total response to the Lord. These words of Jesus at the heart of the New Testament are the proclamation of Jesus' revelation of God as the sole reality for any who would follow the Lord.

This does not mean that the beatitudes were easy for Father Philip; it rather means that they were the other horizon, that still more that ever beckoned him. In the words of Father Philip's favorite poem, "The Four Quartets" by T.S. Eliot:

We shall not cease from exploration
And the end of all our exploring
Will be to arrive where we started
And know the place for the first time.

Father was a religious for almost 61 years, and from a certain optic these last years were the crowning of that total commitment — being completely dependent, having to receive all, trusting absolutely in others for everything.

These virtues did not come naturally to Father Philip. The notes he left behind — the well worn, often annotated copies of the New Testament — all give evidence of his desire to be that true disciple. The poor in spirit, the sorrowing one, the gentle spirit, the hungered after justice, the merciful one, the pure of heart, the peace maker, the bearer of struggle for the sake of justice

How difficult it was to be a disciple, and this Father Philip experienced all his life. He was always the searcher, always looking further; a bit restless, always engaged and wanting to be engaged.

He loved the excitement of Vatican II and the changes it portended, yet he feared he would struggle with his resistance.

One would meet him on the road in the woods and his remark would be: "Do you get it?" When asked, "Get what?" it would be some concern from a recent theological article or guest speaker, something he had been reading, that was causing him great consternation. Once he was reassured that you, too, were living in trust, you too did not really get it, he was encouraged, and perhaps at peace.

Father Philip had been a very successful high school teacher with the Holy Cross Brothers, best known for his musical ability, his choral work, and his work with liturgical choirs.

His heart wanted something more, and responded to that voice as described in his favorite poem, T.S. Eliot's *Four Quartets:*

> *...heard, half heard in the stillness*
> *Between two waves of the sea.*
> *Quick now, here, now, always-*
> *A condition of complete simplicity*

So, Father Philip gave everything and left his much loved polyphony for the Cistercian Plain Song, found our choir a very difficult place to be, yet would never consider not being a part of it because it was where the Lord Jesus called him. Our lack of musical ability, a form of music that was not responsive to his taste, the everydayness of it. That is the cross, he would say, that is where Jesus is to be found.

Father Philip aspired to no position within the community. He even wondered if it was a lack of generosity on his part *not* to desire some place. He loved his book-binding, both the craft, the place and particularly its Patron, Saint Joseph. Many of us, as novices, would be sent to help in the bindery on those days when things were tough and Father Philip with his accepting heart and open spirit would soon lead one from the closed world of temptation to sewing bindings and gluing "supers. "

Father Philip had an expansive spirit, loved things of culture — music, poetry; loved nature and to work in it, bringing it to order; loved good food and Feast Days. He loved life and never wanted to sin against it by refusing it, by refusing to grow.

Yet he always feared something, was concerned about that last great trial, often spoke of death in jest, and in very deep seriousness. Once the time came to be in the infirmary, he wanted to be a good patient. He would be bright and cheerful, calling out his greetings and worried if he was doing all right.

And so he moved into that very long period during which we all came to share his life, never sure if we were intruding or if we were being sufficiently present. Again from his favorite poet:

> And all shall be well and
> All manner of things shall be well
> When the tongues of flame are in-folded
> Into the crowned knot of fire
> And the fire and the rose are one.

During the last 14 months of his life Father Philip was bed-ridden and unable to eat, talk or communicate in any way.

And so the ardent fire of Father Philip's heart and the most perfect of nature's blooms — that is, destruction and total life-became one over the years of being served, waiting, sharing in the mystery of Jesus' dying and rising, not by sacrament only, not by proclaiming the Word as he was ordained to do, but by being a living part of that Word, and calling each of us beyond our insulated selves to care for life in all its ordinariness.

—27 January 1990

It is very appropriate that a priest who had such a deep and articulate love for the Church, as Father Raymond, should be called forth to the fullness of life — into the full gathering of the Church — on Pentecost, a day sometimes referred to as the foundation of the missionary Church. Perhaps that in itself is a sign that the "man got even with God."

It is an even more felicitous chance that gathered to celebrate this Liturgy of Passage are the Novice Directors of the monasteries in the US and one each from Canada and Hong Kong.

Not that Father Raymond would much favor such a meeting, but the reality is that some of his earlier writings had a real influence on many vocations to the monastic life.

And it is a grace to have these monks and nuns present to acknowledge Father Raymond's particular vocation as they reflect on the formation of future generations.

With confidence we can say that there is a whole generation of monks who have been influenced by the *The Man Who Got Even With God*, which is the title of one of Father Raymond's books, and whose historical character, with all his hot-tempered action, is possibly the best description of the author, and may be even a way towards understanding his vocation.

Father Raymond's vocation as a monk was always something of an enigma to me. Perhaps he can best be understood in a very traditional classification of monastic living.

Father Raymond was a penitent. His original choice of life career was to be a member of the Jesuits, and was ordained a priest with them. Within a few years he was dismissed from the Jesuits, something he never even alluded to in his autobiographical writings. Yet it was that event that gave the form and burden to the rest of his long life.

The Gospel text from John (12:23-28) validates the form to which Father Raymond responded, to give his life a direction. Jesus speaks of the seed dying to produce fruit; losing life; hating life so as to have it in all eternity. The last phrases of the Gospel speak of the desire to glorify the Father's name. That is how Father Raymond would describe his life as a priest-monk: Dying, losing, giving glory to God, praising the Father by singing the Office and joining the mission of Jesus by celebrating the Eucharist. He could speak with ease on the meaning of a life based on those principles of praise and union with Jesus.

And in this union with Jesus' redemptive mission he could understand the life-denying harshness of mid-twentieth century Trappist life, and enter with aggressive zeal the heavy manual labor, the rigorous silence, the stringent fasts in a natural climate that only added to the burdens.

The very hardness and harshness added meaning to the penitential life and gave glory to God by its denial and gave form to Father Raymond's life.

Father Raymond labeled himself an "intellectual snob," and he was. He delighted in the well-honed argument that recalled his career as a debater. He loved the fine distinctions of scholastic argument as much as the flowery prose of nineteenth century literature. He was the proud author of 20 books and numerous pamphlets written anonymously, and there is more reason for pride in some of the books than in others.

Father Raymond was culturally interested, more at the level of politics and the sports page than the finer arts. He established strong and lasting personal relationships in which he never hesitated "to pull punches" (his phrase) about the superiority of his positions and ideas. He loved having visitors. He loved writing very long letters of counsel and guidance to a variety of persons. I am ever grateful that I became abbot only after it was necessary to read the outgoing mail.

Father Raymond was ever holy mother Church's ardent apostle; he was faithful to her most minute demands, although with a sure Jesuit logic he could make the distinction for liberty.

It was the Church of the Council of Trent that was his ideal. Vatican II was very difficult for him, as were the many changes introduced into religious life in its wake. They weakened the sureness of the strict regime, a regime that had let narrowness be understood as salvation. Yet as one who knew history he trusted the movement, and he moved from the preacher who proclaimed that one had to earn heaven; had to suffer to be saved; to the little old man who needed help for his elemental needs, and could say with calm conviction that God is good, that mercy is God's love.

Father Raymond had deep family ties. There were three priests in the family and two nuns, and five other children. His care and concern for his nephews and nieces (his brother and sister-in-law having died within a short period) was exceedingly generous. His concern was primarily for their spiritual well-being, and had caused him some pain. He was always direct and demanding to all his relatives and friends regarding their lives within the Church, a directness that strangely endeared him to many, and also separated him from some.

The Eucharist, the Mass, was Father Raymond's life. It was, for him, his life; it was for him his very identity, a sure form of prayer, a way of life. It brought him into an ever deepening awareness of the poverty of Jesus' mission, especially during these last several years when his physical and mental energies were lessened, and he came to realize that God is Love, God is ever generous — we do not get even with God.

What do we see behind the brashness of character, the strong word, the sure critic that was the persona of this self-styled Rasputin? There was a man who knew failure, the person who really could not control, the man who sought out the mercy of God in the rigors of Trappist life because he knew his weakness. There was the priest ever faithful to the Church, always wanting to put on the identity of Christ, there was the penitent knowing that the mercy of God is without bounds, knowing that we do not get even, we only learn to have the freedom to receive.

—4 june 1990

Although the scripture readings were picked for this occasion, in some ways they don't quite fit. Or rather they just say too much. Only the second last phrase of the Gospel (Luke 12:35-40) is realty needed, where it says "be ready".

That, for me, epitomizes Brother Tobias' basic response to life — to all of life — at its various times and seasons. It seems even from his earliest years till the moment before his passage into eternity, all he endeavored to do was to be ready. The intensity of his readiness was witnessed by one of the brothers a day or so before he went forth to the Lord.

As he watched in awe, Brother Tobias was lying on his bed with eyes closed tightly, "punching-out" some unseen aggressor, with short jabs in the air, and a wider swing, all with an intensity that was always Brother Tobias' hallmark.

It may have been the age-old adversary of humankind who was giving Brother a final workout.

He often spoke of the evil spirits' attacks on him. In fact with simplicity and candor, he told the attending physician who cared for his broken hip a couple of years ago, that it was the devil who picked him up and threw him out of the bed. As the story was told a few days later, he not only threw him out of bed, he picked him up and threw him down again. The stories got better with the telling.

Brother Tobias was a late vocation, arriving at Gethsemani's gate when he was 48, seeking to serve God by a life of work and penance, and as he said in his letter of application, "even silence will not be a burden when one's thoughts are on God"

Brother was a constant worker, a hard worker, always with a single-hearted devotion which sometimes had all the evidence of being hard headed self-will or just plain old fashioned dedication — depending on whether you agreed with his way or not.

It was not just in hard work that the single focused strength was in evidence. His life of prayer had the same untrammeled character about it. It was the Eucharist with the brothers, it was the office of our Fathers and Hail Marys, it was a great deal of time before the Blessed Sacrament, time which for years began more than an hour before the rest of the community even thought of rising in the morning. And it was all with an unpretentious faithfulness.

Work and hard work had been Brother Tobias' life since his earliest years. He had been born in Poland and ultimately spent a number of years working at Chrysler Assembly #1 in Hamtramck, Michigan. (Anyone from that general area needs no further description.)

He was an assiduous worker, and was often chosen to be a leader of others in work. Any who experienced his leadership easily understand the nickname "Pharaoh" He gained this when he tried to put order into the lower guest garden known as "Egypt". For years he cared for the Guesthouse, always insisting that the guests deserve a well-made bed. After all it is Christ who is being welcomed. Many a postulant earned his first monastic correction, when the room he helped Brother Tobias clean didn't meet muster.

Brother's initial vocational experience came at the beauty of an early morning Mass in his parish church during the years when he supported his mother and father through their final illness.

This was the only source of brightness in a day filled with many concerns and burdens, and the usual hard work.

It was there in the neighborhood parish that the thought of how beautiful it would be to live in and care for God's house came into Brother's heart. After his mother's death, he prayed, and a series of fortuitous events brought him to Gethsemani's gate.

His monastic life was balanced with the third element of our tradition, *lectio divina* (holy reading.) When not at prayer or work Brother could be found In the Scriptorium, reading his much worn Bible, or in these later years, assiduously following the Pope's latest message in *l'osservatore Romano*, He took much joy and pride in his compatriot John Paul II.

Brother's whole monastic life was lived in that confident expectation and hope of eternal life. As the second reading gave expression to the Apostle Paul's longing to be at home with the Lord — "but whether at home or away, we make it our aim to please the Lord."

With the same confidence Brother Tobias would speak of his longing for heaven, but always willing to remain, if that was the Father's will. His closeness to eternity, his living just this side of the whole world of spirits, was often rewarded by his experience of the Blessed Virgin Mary looking down upon him, encouraging him in his work, being a comfortable presence in his life.

—26 June 1990

Several years ago, in fact a great many years ago, when I was a young professed, I was involved in the common work, which was the renovation of the monastic buildings, replacing the wooden floors and stairwells with bar joists, cement and terrazzo.

One long-term part of the project was re-building stair-wells, and coming behind the welder, it was my job to grind, file and use emery paper on the welds preparing them for painting.

It always seemed to be weather like today — cold and dull. The steel spindles in the stair-railings were also very cold and very dull. Each day after spending a couple of hours grinding and filing, I would ask the master welder if it was sufficient. Generally the response was: "It needs a little more, Frater." And back to grinding, hoping for the bell that sounded the end of the work.

Several months ago the adage — "What goes around, comes around," — was fulfilled in our renovation project. One of the stairwells I worked on was again subject to renovation.

There one morning a local workman with a cutting torch appeared before a section of railing I had worked on assiduously, and in a matter of minutes turned it into scrap metal, and with something of an expression of disdain and superiority he threw it on a pile of scrap.

It did something to me. It gave me a great deal of empathy for Brother Claude and what he so often had suffered in our context.

Brother was an exquisite craftsman of the old world tradition who knew the ways of wood and most everything else, who loved a clean line and a level surface and would work assiduously to obtain it. It generally only took a matter of minutes for some unthinking brother to ruin the beauty under the pretext of a principle of convenience.

And so Brother Claude's asceticism was constant because a community of men, no matter how well-intentioned, often fail to respect the beauty and good order that a master crafts-man perceives. Much of the clean beauty that we now enjoy was executed by Brother Claude, and though he suffered our insensitivity we have gained much by the environment that he has created to assist our journey to God.

Interestingly, with his demand for order and exactness, Brother Claude was always aware of the abberations — the strange knots in a piece of wood, the gnarled twist of a twig, the exquisite coloration in river gravel stones that are spread around the cloister garth.

Something of that beauty that is both less than and more than the ordered and regular, Brother Claude was the person accepting his vocation to order creation, yet with the lightness of heart to see the exquisiteness in the eccentric.

Brother Claude first entered had the Alexian Brothers but not only until he had assisted his brothers and sisters in the care of their father who was blind.

Under the somewhat gruff impression he made, there was always this kindly person, concerned about the well-being of others, reaching out in faithful friendship to any and all who responded to his interests.

Brother Claude knew the groanings and futility of life. He was plagued with health problems, and the side-effects of medications, and the bunglings of inept care. Yet he was appreciative of the thoughtfulness of the medical professionals and never held a grudge for mistakes made.

The monastic context of service in the simple tasks of living came somewhat easily for Brother Claude, though with the common burdens that insensitivity and incomprehension of brothers always brings.

Still, Brother Claude always looked for something more and found delight in the scriptural commentaries from *Expository Times* and in the stories of persons who experienced the beneficent intervention of the divine in a situation that seemed hopeless — the cure that was extraordinary, the conversion that was completely unexpected.

Though there was something of a convenient fit of Brother Claude and monastic culture — that familiarity which both respected discipline and expected it to be followed by all — he also knew how to celebrate it among friends.

Still, the reality of the monk's aloneness and radical dependence on God alone for life was always there.

There is nothing he would have loved more than to have had an apprentice in whom he could have imbued a spirit and love of order and beauty and good functioning. Yet, though he patiently trained many, there were none to whom he could pass his mantle. The terrible solitude of the monk!

Brother Claude stands alone. He has only the poverty of himself and the hope that he may be with his Brother the Lord Jesus—whose name he believed in; whose love he tried to share with others in however awkward a form.

In reality, whether it be the sharing of the delight in the functional beauty of a bird in flight, or the extraordinary grace in another's life, Brother wanted but one thing, as the closing words of our Gospel say — to make known the name of the Lord, so that others may know the love "with which you have loved me "

There is something fitting about having to separate the burial service from the Mass liturgy for Brother Claude (I am sure if he were with us he would have some comment on doing something like this, and how it should have been done in another manner).

Though he spent so much of himself bringing order from there was always that love of something a little different — you know how true beauty is in that tiniest irregularity that accentuates the order; the evolution of a species is that eccentric particle in the well ordered orbit about the nucleus. So Brother in his order, was always responsive to that Spirit that blows where it will, always just a little askew.

—14 February 1993

"Lord, we do not know where You are going; how can we know the way?" This Gospel text may have been one that haunted Brother Giovanni since one often had the impression that his concern was for an ideal that was far beyond the world of simple reality. Reality was a bit too harsh for his very sensitive heart, so he longed for that perfect space and that perfect time where order and tranquillity were the way of life that was given.

Obviously monasticism offered something of that ideal form and Brother Giovanni gave himself up to realizing that form with all the singleness of heart and purpose that he was capable of. He was an example to us, not only in the generosity of his service be it at the computer, the shoe shop, at welcoming guests, or as servant in the refectory, but more particularly in his frequent private prayer in church, his punctuality at community prayer. He had a love for liturgy, but always a liturgy fulfilled with a certain dignity and serenity, a perfect liturgy.

But this perfect form of monastic life was being imposed on a life that had not been fully accepted, a life that had some of the inevitable mistakes, a life that had demands and responsibilities that called for acceptance and the complications of a reality that didn't fit an ideal form. Brother was more aware of the ideal form than the reality that had to be accepted.

Then monastic living, especially in its day-to-day reality of post-Vatican II, seemingly lost much of the orderliness and security that had been its mythical past. Because in actuality, monasticism in all ages is a Gospel-living only insofar as it is based on reality, the reality that Jesus offers us in the closing phrases of our Gospel and it is the only way to life that Jesus Himself showed us: "I am the way, and the truth, and the life; no one comes to the Father but by me."

And when we look at the life of Jesus, as this liturgical season brings us to do, what is it that we see? In His ultimate moment, in His going forth into death, the specific experiences were of the absence of God, even of the sense of abandonment

117

by God; and the experience of the enormity of human suffering. The hiddenness of God and the profundity of human suffering is the only reality. It was against and within these experiences that Jesus struggled as He moved faithfully toward his death in obedience and love. It is in this same reality that each of us is called to work out his life.

The working out is a moving forward into the depth of this mystery which often becomes even less ordered, more confused — the road is never straight and empty of traffic. Brother Giovanni's road had the inevitable wrong turns and it was these that he wanted to put in order — or have someone else put them in order for him. And since monasticism no longer offered the passive security of a way that cannot go wrong, in his moments of discouragement, confusion and depression, he accepted an offer to be cared for, saved from the harshness of monastic community, and live with certain of life's amenities without the burdens: A temptation that would be difficult for any of us. And he saw it as a way to put in order some of the past he had left unacknowledged.

We gather today with fond memories of Brother Giovanni, who was an example for each of us, we gather with one of his daughters and a grandson who have always showed him such love and support, and we all pray that the peace and order that he longed for are now his. And we must learn from him, as he would want us to. Though the Father's house has many mansions, it is only in following Jesus through the reality of accepting life, all of life, its burdens and confusions, and the reality of always being called further into the mystery of the life of God, the mystery that recognizes the existence of God and the depths of human suffering, a reality of faith which is founded on Jesus' prayer on the cross. It is only there that life is finally ordered.

We remember Giovanni as we break this bread and drink from the cup, aware that in celebrating this Eucharist we all share the one life of the Lord Jesus, which unites us all, which is the sole source of hope, which is the order of the universe.

—2 April 1993

118

I should make something of an apology, or confession, why we are in this very, very hot church on this afternoon.

Certainly if Father Anastasius would have had his way, it would not he nearly so hot. He loved it air-conditioned. I admit I pulled rank on him and turned the air-conditioning off. That is not to say, he is now getting even, but I must confess it as my fault.

When a brother dies, it gives us an opportunity to reflect on a monk's life in the context of the Gospel, to find that encouragement that will lead each of us deeper into the call of discipleship.

Before Anastasius came to Gethsemani he was very much involved in the Apostolate of the Enthronement of the Sacred Heart, which always used this text from today's gospel ("for I am gentle and lowly of heart, and you will find rest for your souls, for my yoke is easy and my burden is light" Matt. 11: 25-30) as foundational for its whole theology.

I think the text, too, was the optic of Father Anastasius's way of discipleship. Just taking the yoke, grasping the burden, was his way of engaging himself in the way he lived life. It also reflected St. Benedict's rule of looking to "hardships and difficulties." That was very much Father Anastasius's way

He simply would say: "Frater, you just got to do it." That was his word of encouragement for whatever difficulty one brought to him. Father Anastasius' hardships and difficulties just went with life. Things had to he completed exactly, no matter how difficult nor how hard, whether it was getting a finish on a paint job, buffing a piece of metal, welding a straight head, and above all, making sure his helper got the grinding nice and smooth. All were of equal importance, the same perfection and single- heartedness was also the principle for executing the chant, reading and studying theology — single-hearted dedication almost oblivious to any amelioration. You just got in there and did it. That was the way one was a disciple.

Our first reading from Isaias (25: 6a, 7,9) with its picture of an eschatalogical banquet that has a Eucharistic connotation, reminds us of the centrality of the priesthood in Father Anastasius' life. It was his great love. To individually celebrate Mass with its immediacy was the heart of his life.

Vatican II's changes were difficult for him. As Master of the Brothers for many years he had opportunities to exercise his priestly ministry. There was a time when the number of Professed brothers in the Community was the largest portion of the Community. In fact, Father Alan tells me at one time there were 99 Professed lay brothers when Father Anastasius was Father Master.

It was for these that he prepared conferences, and gave direction. He was there to help with sensitive community relations, and often was caught in the center, between the Abbot and the Brother. This was a source of tension for him. Yet it was always something that Father Anastasius bore with his harsh determination, kept him uncritically faithful to his Superiors, but often burdened for the sake of the brothers.

His many years as Father Master, as Subprior and Prior, indicate how sound his counsel was. He was someone who could keep a confidence, someone with a pastoral sense. Though he went at life so strongly, he knew how to look for the way to help a Brother in time of difficulty.

One of the recurring metaphors he used in his afternoon conferences was about the bent chassis, this was how he symbolized human nature affected by original sin.

All the brothers who managed to stay awake at that hour of the day became very knowledgeable concerning the intricacies of straightening a chassis, how the fact is that it really never is the same.

Our reading from Romans (8:35-37,39), that nothing can really come between us and the love of Christ, was certainly Father Anastasius' message and example. His zeal was single-hearted in its direction, unbending in its exactness, and with little relief by any sense of humor — he really didn't seem to have any. Father Anastasius lived totally for God. There was nothing that would keep him from the one thing necessary, the love of beauty as a violinist, the love of Family, the care of his Mother which he had to leave to others, his own desire and admiration for family life. All these, he very willingly surrendered for the sake of the Lord Jesus, with the simplicity with which he did everything: "You just got to get in there and do it."

When his weakness first confined him to the Infirmary, I asked him one day what he missed most of all. He said he missed having a welding rod in his hand. After a little further reflection, he told me some of his happiest days were days when he executed these stainless steel crosses, polishing them to a high glimmer, and having others enjoy the beauty that they were.

I think if there were some type or contest to name "Mr. Gethsemani Trappist" of the last half century, the race would he close, but certainly there is little doubt that Father Anastasius would he one of the finalists. The unique blend and same singlehearted devotion, brought a sensitive love for the Liturgy — a conviction regarding the injunction of the Rule of Benedict: "We are truly monks when we earn our living by the work of our hands . "

—7 July 1993

There was something very simple and direct about Father David's way of living the Gospel. It seems it goes back to his youngest days. His sisters spoke of the desire he had to be a priest as even a very young boy, and this was the one compelling desire that seemed to change his life.

As a young man he joined the Scarborough Foreign Missions, a counterpart of Maryknoll, and went to China where he worked mightily to master the language so he could proclaim the Gospel to this people.

By the time he had mastered the language, however, he was in an internment camp, established by the Japanese in China. It was here he encountered for the first time live Trappist monks. They got him in some trouble, since he endeavored to help them in their involvement in a black market of getting food into that camp. Unfortunately, Father David would up getting caught in trying to hold up his part of the bargain. Ultimately he was freed, and ended up under house arrest, but then soon came back to Canada.[4]

That phase of his life, so to speak, being finished, he headed off into a whole new district. He went to Santo Domingo. He had a whole new language to learn, and a whole new culture to become familiar with, and so he did.

In one of those rare moments when Father would acknowledge something of his personal past, he said his experience in Santo Domingo and the petty dictatorships there was far worse than anything in the internment camp.

Father David finally came to the Trappists and entered Gethsemani in December of 1957.

At the time of Father David's 50th anniversary of priesthood in 1989, trying to have him recollect on his varied career, one realized that this person never really had much self-consideration in any of these contexts where life was lived rather on the outer limits of endurance.

He never recollected the hardships or burdens or the sufferings he had. His memories were really of how the internment

122

camps broke down the barriers between Christians, broke down the barriers between clerics and nuns and lay people, and allowed a life of simple Christian fellowship, which was a life he related to very easily.

We knew something of this same self-effacing person in seeing his presence in our midst, the way he served the brethren, the way he received the guests and retreatants over many years with a great deal of self-sacrifice, giving himself constantly in that ministry; the way that he was part of our simple work project.

There were those many occasions when he without question would respond to a simple request to do something for the sake of the Order, for the sake of the Community.

Without any complication, for example, he simply packed his bags and went to Mexico to be a chaplain for a new foundation of nuns there. With the same simplicity and directness, he went off to Chile, again to immerse himself in a foreign culture, to live with simplicity and directness, doing what he was asked to do.

And for years he served the nuns at Wrentham, again always self-effacing, without really considering himself.

Ultimately, as his health weakened while he worked with the nuns of Wrentham, he expressed to me over and over again his desire to be with his brethren because he found community such a real support, such a way to come to realize the fullness of God's kingdom. I doubt if in all of Father David's life if he ever entertained the question: "What's in it for me?" He simply moved into whatever he was asked to do, and did it with the talents he had, and so moved on through life.

One can't help but think it was those many years of self-effacing service that allowed him these last few months to be so often resting so securely and peacefully here in the presence of the Blessed Sacrament

Father David had lived so uncomplicatedly during so many years of his life. He was someone who was always interested in the brethren, interested in the life of the Community, always had a sense of humor that could poke a bit of fun at a brother, and always had ability to laugh at himself and his own not infrequent faux pas. Perhaps a danger in a large community like ours has been to take someone like Father David for granted; yet in some ways that is what he wanted, and as we all know, those who live so simply are the real backbone of our whole community.

—27 August 1993

[4]Father Timothy Kelly himself is Father David's fellow Canadian.

FATHER VIANNEY WOLFER

One of the many lessons I did not learn from Father Vianney — though he tried valiantly to teach me, indeed, as he endeavored with so much effort to teach me theology, rubrics, how to wash fruitcake pans, and so many other things — but one thing I never learned was how to put my two little fingers in my mouth and blow the steamboat whistle. I've tried but it doesn't work.

During the last several months, Father Vianney has seemed more and more free to blow that whistle. Really, he has just been more and more free. Some days ago, in the middle of the morning work I met him leaning on the wall in front of the library resting on his way back to the bakery after having obtained a new can of cleanser. He told me that he wanted to have a motorcycle for doing such errands. In fact, the one thing he wanted to do before going to heaven, was to ride a motorcycle around the shops building and then off down the road. Then he laughed with that gleeful laugh: "That would be great fun!"

This was Father Vianney — the one filled with the freedom of a child of God, yet so concerned about the many little things that make life function properly. He spent the last days telling the novices where the candles are for particular functions. He was always concerned about who would open the west transept door at 3 a. m. in the morning. He wondered who would dust the scriptorium, and we all know — no one.

Perhaps the last line of our Gospel tells us who Father Vianney was in our midst —" I have made your name known to them, and I will make it known, so that the love with which you have loved me may he in them... "

His whole life was centered on that single-hearted love of God under the symbol of the Sacred Heart, that love at the Church, the Eucharist, the priesthood.

His many years of assignment to the Guest Retreat house for priests and for laymen, gave him that providential opportunity, as did the generations of monastic theology students.

He taught many of us the seminary course in theology but more than the text book theology there was that great respect and love of the Church and the Church as teacher, that he endeavored to imbue in his students. It was this fidelity to the Church as teacher that brought him through the many changes of the Vatican II era. Though he saw so many things that he loved transformed, changed or destroyed, Father Vianney never faltered in his resolve that the message of Jesus was being proclaimed with ever more clarity.

Though he was generally most unwilling to acknowledge it, he was a Doctor of Theology.

In his usual way of poking fun at himself, he would tell the story about his Theology degree from Fribourg. His professor called him in at the time of the final exam and pointed out the incompletion of his work, propositions he had failed to consider, and just the many lacuna in what he had done.

Father Vianney was quite sure that the work was unacceptable. But then with laughter in his telling, he would quote the Latin phrase of the professor who said that the theology was weak, but because of friendship he would give him his degree.

Whether the theology was lacking or not doesn't matter, but none of us doubts the friendship that surely was between Father and the professor, because his manner of relating to all of us, or just to everyone, was as a friend.

Regarding his time in Fribourg, more than the friendship of the theology professor, Father Vianney delighted in telling stories of the beauties of the Swiss Alps, the joy of skiing, the exhilaration of the mountain air, the majesty and beauty of God that nature so revealed.

Yet the spirituality he experienced seemed to be very different from the clean, bright exhilaration of Swiss mountain air. His seemed to be the strength of will that fulfilled with devotion every small point and big point of any and every expression of piety and of life itself. Always with uncomplaining will and always looking for a way to do still more.

And so whether it was washing fruitcake pans while others idled, or praying the office of the Blessed Virgin that no longer was a requirement, Father Vianney did it with an unobtrusive faithfulness that never judged a monk who burdened him because of his thoughtlessness, or even something more negative.

And though he longed for all of us to know his joy in being faithful, he never condemned our lack of fervor, but rather encouraged the slightest evidence of life that was in us.

We could go on and on about his Eucharistic devotions his sense of God's mercy through the Sacred Heart devotion, his love of ministering God's mercy and compassion in the Sacrament of Penance, and all those little evidences these last days that Eternity was breaking through and he even knew it — prostrating beside his bed when the call of Eternity came, praying the Glorious Mysteries because he knew the time of glory was at hand: In celebrating his last Eucharist with us on that day which is so very particular to our own Community, the Feast of the Dedication of the Church of Gethsemani.

Our Brother, our Father, has gone from us, but we each know a friend who now is in the presence of the Lord, who would encourage each of us at the least evidence of our good will, saying: "Come on, big bozo, if I can do it, you can do it! "

Listen, I am sure we will hear a motorcycle roaring around the shops building!

—17 November 1993

"No, it was for this that I came to this hour, Father glorify thy name." (Jn. 12: 23-28)

Possibly it was just the first word, the "No," in its simple strong directness that reminds me of Brother Victor. It is said with firmness and absoluteness so that there is just no other way. It could have been "Yes" that was spoken. In some sense it makes no difference. Either way it is just as absolute and there is no room for the opposite or especially for the gray area between.

From another perspective, our first reading, from the Book of Job, epitomizes Brother Victor. Not so much the precise reading, though that too has Victor written on it — the words being chiseled into rock with an iron tool; and the one who would stand for his witness was God Himself; that is Victor at his best! There were few of Brother's statements or opinions that did not have this seal of omniscience that God would give witness to. In some ways just the whole character of Job is something of Victor's — not the reputation Job has for patience! Patience was not one of Brother's strong points. In some ways it wasn't Job's either. But Job standing fast in his innocence, despite what his friends claimed, reminds one of Brother. The last chapters of the book, when God answers Job and vindicates Job's refusal to accept the friends' accusations as proper, is something that Victor could delight in. Though God still does not answer Job directly, He reminds him that God is God and the power is in God's hands. Victor would love such an answer and defend it with all his being and tell you, "You better believe it".

His first awareness of Trappist monastic life was through the book "The Man Who Got Even WIth God". A very appropriate book and the title is a fitting commentary on his vocation. He anguished over life and the "why" of it all after his experience in the Marines. And he ultimately made the great gamble with God, I expect with a certain amount of, "I dare you, God," in it — something on the line of, "O.K. you want it all; here you are. Now what are you going to do with it!"

His time in the Marines was most memorable, probably for the Marines too! The military discipline, the rugged life, the purposefulness of it all, the camaraderie of like minded men were things that attracted Victor. Actually the war was over when Victor reached Japan and his service in the army of occupation. He always told stories of collecting the K-ration of chocolate and breaking it into little pieces to give to the children. This story is much easier to believe than the one about shooting a person when on guard duty that was ultimately the reason why he could not return to the seminary.

The Marine motto, "Semper fidelis" is appropriate for Brother Victor. He was always faithful. A bit eclectic in many areas of just what to be faithful to, but once the choice to be faithful was established nothing could change it. It was the same be it faithfulness to a work project, a friendship or his monastic commitment. Somewhere down deep, he would say yes, and nothing would ever deter him. But that same absolute commitment had its downside. If he decided against a project, a person, a religious expression, the same unflinching determination was evidenced.

These last several months we have come to know the hard won fruits of that "semper fidelis". First it was Alzheimer's and the impossibility of keeping the cheese schedule, and the retirement which wasn't easy for one who had run his own life, centered on work. Then came the cancer and the resultant anemia and kidney disorder which dictated a move to the infirmary.

The directness of Jesus' response in the Gospel, the "No/Yes" of accepting the last hour, is a real image of Brother Victor. So too the closing words of the second reading, "There is nothing in all creation that can separate us from the love of God in Christ, Jesus our Lord": Not the brown habit or the cheese plant or the justice for those who work for us; not the Brother's Office not the brothers who were his confidants who chose to leave, nor a whole changed ethos in the community. In the end all that mattered is this love that we celebrate in this Eucharist, the bread and wine of a life spent for the sake of the Father, for our sakes, as the food of eternal life. As Brother Victor would say when pushed about his vocation, "There is only one reason and it has nothing to do with the brothers or the place, it has to do with God".

—10 July 1995

BROTHER GUERRIC PLANTE

Several months ago in conversation with Brother Guerric he assured me that he was going to live twenty years more. We won't go into the context of the conversation of how it developed that far, but it reveals something about him. He loved life. At the same time, there was an intriguing mystery about his own life. There was a hiddenness, a secretiveness, something being guarded, something that at least I was never able to glimpse.

Brother Guerric was a presence in the Community, just by his size and his acute awareness of everything and anything around him. There was a sensitivity toward persons, places and things. He perceived the taste of the individual spices in the fruit cake, the delicate bouquet of a wine, the unique play of a cloth or grain of wood. But in some sense, this sensitivity almost overwhelmed him. It came at him too strongly. Though he always offered an unperturbed personality, one could sense a deep fear of being overwhelmed. How to move from the delicate sense perceptions to a life that had to be lived day by day, a life of just putting one foot ahead of another? This seemed very difficult for Brother. He had perceptions and visions and perhaps hopes. But he did not know how to give these the life that had the perfection he seemed to perceive as all important. This, I think, nearly overwhelmed him. Somewhere deep within, there was a question, how to know the Spirit who seems not to be freed just by constraining the body? Did he really perceive that the mortification of the flesh and emotional deprivation are not the means to spiritual enlightenment but may constrict the soul? Was he able to accept being human, this person who gave the appearance of being too human?

As a twenty year old college student from Kalamazoo, Michigan, Guerric visited Gethsemani and then entered forty-six years ago. He was involved in life. Very soon he was put in charge of the vegetable gardens which, on those days before the mail order business, were a source of life for the community. Some would say that being in charge meant he did put the food on the table. He proved to be very innovative in his ideas of organization. For many years he was involved in the food service for the retreatants. That meant scheduled food preparation with the help of other brothers for about seventy hardy guests three times a day. Of course the chef had to taste

130

his product and undoubtedly that is where some of the first setbacks were experienced in the never-ending battle with his weight.

Brother Guerric was also the monastery baker for many years and took great pride in the fruitcakes he produced. The disciplined structure of the recipe and the coordinated work that always produced a good product was something he rightfully took pride in. It was a time of real joy for him when he was asked to spend several weeks at a monastery in Brazil helping to develop a fruitcake. The joy of a new country and the awareness of making do with what was available brought to life some of Brother's old talents and interests. It was a joy for him to be able to share his knowledge and experience so that others could have more life.

During the days of Vatican II when our community was hesitatingly moving into the era of dialogue, we became aware of a whole other side of Brother as he handled community meetings and would calm troubled waters with some word of Native American Wisdom or Guerric shrewdness. It was this time in his life that the sociability of Brother was more in evidence. He cared for the retired Abbot, James Fox. By the way, Abbot James would be one hundred years old today. Brother Guerric cared for him with the devotion of a loving son — something that took a certain amount of virtue on both sides. His concern for those in material need especially in the local area and his work for the monastery with the Sisters who help us to be responsive to the people in the area was a part of his growing social conscientiousness. This heightened his interest in local politics and the intricate relations of the neighbouring families and their many kin.

It was during this time too that Brother became more aware of Thomas Merton and his writings. Another of those coincidences. Today is the anniversary of Father Louis' entrance into the monastic life and his death in 1968. Guerric delighted in sharing stories about Merton that received a special twist in the telling. The interest in Merton touched Brother Guerric in ways related to his monastic life. Merton speaks often of the true self, of the only self that can relate to the Spirit. Merton speaks eloquently of the importance of knowing this true self. That is whom Guerric wanted to know. How to do it without letting anyone else in was perhaps his difficulty. A difficulty that is not unique to Guerric.

In his journey to know the true Guerric he began to own

his Native American roots with the joy of someone discovering a new world. He had the opportunities to enter into some of the spiritual traditions of his people that began to give him a better definition of self. As for all of us, the road to self-knowledge, the narrow way, is arduous. It is boring. It is constant. There is no quick fix which Brother, like so many of us, had a tendency to look for in all the trinkets of the electronic age and new theories in our world of infinite choices. But the inner restlessness seemed to remain. The clutter of his living space perhaps symbolized the clutter of his interior solitude. Clutter in our living space, in our souls, always makes life uncomfortable.

Yet his love of life had him reach out more. He participated in twelve-step programs and he found new courage and wisdom in his talks with Dr. Jane Thibault. He was reading one of her books in the hospital. The marker was left at a quotation from Paul to the Philippians, chapter three. "I believe nothing can happen that will outweigh the supreme advantage of knowing Christ Jesus my Lord... All I want to know Christ and the power of his resurrection and to share his sufferings by reproducing the pattern of his death."

It seems that he was taken at his word. His death was in his awareness. He had asked that his sister be informed of his condition. Something he had never done before. He was insistent in asking for prayers. This was not the Guerric we knew. We thrust that now he knows the fullness of all life.

Each of our lives is a mystery. A mystery that offers a few glimpses. the little vignettes we saw of Brother Guerric had a quality of desiring life. We gather to remember Brother by sharing in a banquet of life. I am sure that of all the images of eternity the ones of it as banquet appealed to Brother. The banquet we have come to share is the source of all life, the very life of Jesus. In sharing this we remain in the one life the unites all of us through the life of Jesus to Brother Guerric who lives by that same life.

—10 December 1996